THE HISTORY OF CUBA

Clifford L. Staten

The Greenwood Histories of the Modern Nations
Frank W. Thackeray and John E. Findling, Series Editors

GREENWOOD PRESS
Westport, Connecticut • London

Library of Congress Cataloging-in-Publication Data

Staten, Clifford, L.
    The history of Cuba / Clifford L. Staten.
        p. cm.—(The Greenwood histories of the modern nations, ISSN 1096–2905)
    Includes bibliographical references and index.
    ISBN 0–313–31690–2 (alk. paper)
    1. Cuba—History—20th century. 2. Cuba—History—1810–1899. I. Title. II. Series.
F1787.S76 2003
972.91—dc21   2002035334

British Library Cataloguing in Publication Data is available.

Library of Congress Catalog Card Number: 2002035334
ISBN: 0–313–31690–2
ISSN: 1096–2905

First published in 2003

Greenwood Press, 88 Post Road West, Westport, CT 06881
An imprint of Greenwood Publishing Group, Inc.
www.greenwood.com

Printed in the United States of America

∞™

The paper used in this book complies with the
Permanent Paper Standard issued by the National
Information Standards Organization (Z39.48–1984)

10 9 8 7 6 5 4 3 2 1

Contents

Series Foreword

The Greenwood Histories of the Modern Nations series is intended to provide students and interested laypeople with up-to-date, concise, and analytical histories of many of the nations of the contemporary world. Not since the 1960s has there been a systematic attempt to publish a series of national histories, and, as series editors, we believe that this series will prove to be a valuable contribution to our understanding of other countries in our increasingly interdependent world.

Over thirty years ago, at the end of the 1960s, the Cold War was an accepted reality of global politics, the process of decolonization was still in progress, the idea of a unified Europe with a single currency was unheard of, the United States was mired in a war in Vietnam, and the economic boom of Asia was still years in the future. Richard Nixon was president of the United States, Mao Tse-tung (not yet Mao Zedong) ruled China, Leonid Brezhnev guided the Soviet Union and Harold Wilson was prime minister of the United Kingdom. Authoritarian dictators still ruled most of

Latin America, the Middle East was reeling in the wake of the Six-Day War, and Shah Reza Pahlavi was at the height of his power in Iran. Clearly, the past thirty years have been witness to a great deal of historical change, and it is to this change that this series is primarily addressed.

With the help of a distinguished advisory board, we have selected nations whose political, economic, and social affairs mark them as among the most important in the early years of the twenty-first century, and for each nation we have found an author who is recognized as a specialist in the history of that nation. These authors have worked most cooperatively with us and with Greenwood Press to produce volumes that reflect current research on their nation and that are interesting and informative to their prospective readers.

The importance of a series such as this cannot be underestimated. As a superpower whose influence is felt all over the world, the United States can claim a "special" relationship with almost every other nation. Yet many Americans know very little about the histories of the nations with which the United States relates. How did they get to be the way they are? What kind of political systems have evolved there? What kind of influence do they have in their own region? What are the dominant political, religious, and cultural forces that move their leaders? These and many other questions are answered in the volumes of this series.

The authors who have contributed to this series have written comprehensive histories of their nations, dating back to prehistoric time in some cases. Each of them, however, has devoted a significant portion of the book to events of the past thirty years, because the modern era as contributed the most to contemporary issues that have an impact on U.S. policy. Authors have made an effort to be as up-to-date as possible so that readers can benefit from the most recent scholarship and a narrative that includes very recent events.

In addition to the historical narrative, each volume in this series contains an introductory overview of the country's geography, political institutions, economic structure and cultural attributes. This is designed to give readers a picture of the nation as it exists in the contemporary world. Each volume also contains additional chapters that add interesting and useful detail to the historical narrative. One chapter is a thorough chronology of important historical events, making it easy for readers to follow the flow of a particular nation's history. Another chapter features biographical sketches of the nation's most important figures in order to humanize some of the individuals who have contributed to the historical development of their nation. Each volume also contains a comprehensive bibliography, so that those readers whose interest has been sparked may find out more about the nation and its history. Finally, there is a carefully prepared topic and person index.

Readers of these volumes will find them fascinating to read and useful in understanding the contemporary world and the nations that comprise it. As series editors, it is our hope that this series will contribute to a heightened sense of global understanding as we embark on a new century.

Frank W. Thackeray and John E. Findling
Indiana University Southeast

Acknowledgments

In writing a book such as this, I am indebted to a vast academic literature on Cuba and scores of excellent scholars who have studied and written about the island. I would like to thank my secretaries Mary Ann Braden, Leslie Deal and Brigette Colligan, who kept a watchful eye over my daily schedule and gave me the time to complete the book. Frank Thackeray and John E. Findling of Indiana University Southeast, Kevin Ohe of Greenwood Press, Steven Long, and Emma Bailey of Westchester Book Services have done an excellent and meticulous job of editing various versions of the manuscript. Indiana University also provided me with a grant to conduct some research in Cuba in the summer of 2001. I would also like to thank several other people who have contributed to this book in many different ways: my life-long friend Boone Chaffin, Clair Matz of Marshall University, Neal Tate of the University of North Texas, my friend from graduate school and Foreign Service officer George Aldridge, Stephanie Bower and Tim Ambrose of Indiana University Southeast, Allen Maxwell of Indiana University Kokomo, Robert Harding of Lynchburg College and John Gilderbloom of the University of Louisville. I especially want to thank my wife Shannon and my children Joshua, Ryan and Anna for their patience with me while writing this book and my mother Nancy, who has always been my biggest fan. Finally, this book is dedicated to the loving memory of my father, Melvin "Tippy" Staten.

Timeline of Historical Events

1250	Taino Indians arrive in Cuba
1492	Christopher Columbus lands in Cuba
1514	First Spanish settlements established
1515	Santiago de Cuba becomes the capital of the colony
1518	Hernán Cortés leaves for Mexico from Cuba
1522	First African slaves brought to Cuba
1607	Havana declared capital of Cuba
1700	Tobacco becomes the primary export
1728	University of Havana founded
1762	British capture Havana;
	Liberalized trade and commercial and maritime laws established

1763   Spain regains control of Havana

1765   Spanish begin liberalizing trade and commercial and
            maritime laws

1791   Slave uprising in Haiti eliminates main competitor to
            Cuban sugar

1800   Sugar becomes primary export

1837   First railroad built

1838–1880   Modernization of sugar industry in Cuba

1868–1878   First war of independence (Ten Years' War)

1879   Slavery comes to an end

1890   Growing Cuban economic dependence on the United
            States

1895–1898   Second war of independence;

            Economic infrastructure destroyed

1895   José Martí killed in battle and becomes national hero

1898   Battleship USS *Maine* blown up in Havana Harbor;

            President William McKinley offers to purchase Cuba
            from Spain;

            United States declares war on Spain and intervenes
            in Cuban war of independence;

            U.S. armed forces refuse to allow Cubans to take part
            in Spanish surrender in Santiago;

            Peace Treaty signed in Paris with no Cubans invited

1898–1902   U.S. military occupation

1901   Platt Amendment imposed on Cuba

1902   Cuban independence

1903   U.S. naval base at Guantánamo Bay established

1906–1909   U.S. military occupation

1912   U.S. military intervention

1917–1923   U.S. military intervention

1933   Overthrow of the Machado dictatorship

1934	Platt Amendment repudiated
1940	Second constitution proclaimed
1952	*Golpe* by Fulgencio Batista
1953	Fidel Castro attacks barracks at Moncada
1956	Castro and followers land in Oriente Province
1956–1958	Castro wages guerrilla war from Sierra Maestra while underground guerrillas wage war in the cities
1959	Batista flees and Castro arrives triumphantly in Havana; First agrarian reform law passed
1959–1961	Struggle for control of revolution
1960	Large companies nationalized
1961	Bay of Pigs invasion; U.S. trade embargo of Cuba announced
1962	Missile crisis
1964–1970	Radical experiment
1965	The Popular Socialist Party is reorganized as the Communist Party of Cuba by Castro
1967	Ernesto "Che" Guevara killed in Bolivia
1968	Small businesses nationalized; Soviet invasion of Czechoslovakia
1972	Cuba joins the Council for Mutual Economic Assistance trading block
1975	First Communist Party of Cuba Congress held; Cuban troops sent to Angola
1979	Sixth Non-Aligned Summit meeting held in Havana
1980	More than 100,000 Cubans leave for the United States from Mariel
1986–1990	Rectification process
1989	Collapse of East European communism
1990–1995	Special Period

1991   Collapse of the Soviet Union

1992   Torricelli Act passed

1993   Legalization of the U.S. dollar

1995   Direct foreign investment allowed;

            Growing importance of tourism

1996   Helms-Burton Act passed

1998   Pope John Paul II visits Cuba

1999   Cuba celebrates fortieth anniversary of the revolution

2002   Former president Jimmy Carter visits the island

1

Cuba and Its People

When Americans hear the word "Cuba," many thoughts, sounds and images come to mind: the U.S. embargo, a bearded Fidel Castro in army fatigues, the song "Guantanamera," Teddy Roosevelt and the Rough Riders, Ernest Hemingway, *mojitos*, classic automobiles, the missile crisis, the Bay of Pigs, cigars, rum, sugar cane, the mafia, gambling, *I Love Lucy*, the Malecon, raft people braving the shark-infested waters of the Straits of Florida, Little Havana and many others. News from Cuba and discussions of the relationship between Cuba and the United States dominate the media in Miami and are never far from the front pages of the major U.S. newspapers on any given day. During presidential elections in the United States, both the Democratic and Republican candidates pay homage to the Cuban American community in Florida. They reiterate their support for the U.S. embargo against the island while taking note of Florida's important electoral college votes. Even in the post–Cold War era small or seemingly insignificant events concerning Cuba have a tendency to escalate and directly affect the

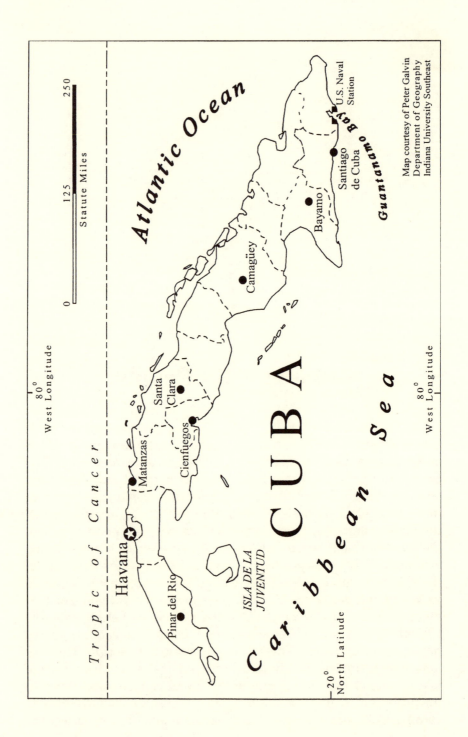

Atlantic Ocean

CUBA

Caribbean Sea

Tropic of Cancer

Havana

Matanzas

Santa Clara

Cienfuegos

Pinar del Rio

ISLA DE LA JUVENTUD

Camagüey

Bayamo

Santiago de Cuba

U.S. Naval Station

Guantanamo Bay

80°
West Longitude

80°
West Longitude

20°
North Latitude

Statute Miles

0   125   250

Map courtesy of Peter Galvin
Department of Geography
Indiana University Southeast

United States. A case in point was the frenzied media coverage of the struggles of Elian Gonzalez, the small Cuban boy who became the center of an international tug-of-war between Cuba and the Cuban American community in Miami. This is a clear illustration of how what should have been a low-profile "nonevent" became a major international story that mobilized Cuban American groups in southern Florida, dominated debate in the U.S. Congress, forced the U.S. attorney general to become involved and directly affected a presidential campaign.

President Bill Clinton once characterized U.S. relations with Cuba as a "terrible family feud." For better and for worse, Cuba and the United States have developed these intimate family ties since the middle of the nineteenth century. Within the framework of these intimate ties, the theme of U.S. hegemony (a form of dominance) over the island and its people is the primary historical perspective. This was achieved not only through direct military, political, diplomatic and economic means, but also through cultural and social interactions. It is important to point out that hegemony implies some consent by the Cubans. American values were transmitted via business practices, tourism, movies, radio, newspapers, advertisements, music, consumer goods, education, protestant missionaries and sports. These values fell on a receptive people, especially at the time of Cuban independence from Spain. Spain represented backwardness and the United States represented progress and civilization. Spanish hegemony was replaced by U.S. hegemony. Even after Fidel Castro's revolution and the rejection of U.S. dominance, it is these values that continue to tie Cuba and the United States together. Cubans are very proud of the major accomplishments of the revolution—cradle-to-grave healthcare, social security and free education for all—but they still tend to measure their progress or lack thereof by the United States.

Although about one-tenth of the Cuban population has fled to the United States since 1959, emigration has been occurring since the middle of the 1800s. The cigar industry that developed in Key West, Jacksonville, Tampa and Ocala is a direct result of Cuban immigration in the late 1800s and early 1900s. In addition to sharing a common people, Cubans and Americans share the love of cars, movies, jazz, Coca-Cola and baseball. The United States brought baseball to Cuba and it quickly became its national pastime in the early 1900s. Players in the U.S. winter league came to Cuba and played on racially integrated teams prior to their integration in the United States. Noted historian Louis A. Pérez Jr. points out that integrated baseball in Cuba helped pave the way for the integration of baseball in the United States. Baseball continues to be a source of national pride today with the Cuban national team considered to be one of the best in the world. Cuban ballparks are always full and watching a baseball game in Cuba is not much different than watching one in the United States. Traveling throughout the island one sees scores of kids playing baseball in fields and alleys and on the side streets—not that different than what one sees every spring and summer in the United States.

THE PEOPLE

Cubans are passionate, gregarious, resourceful, hard working and full of life. With three-fourths of its population of 11,096,400 people living in cities, Cuba is primarily an urban society. Life in the larger cities, such as Havana, Santiago and Camagüey, tends to revolve around the porches, balconies and verandas of the houses or apartment-style living spaces. Kids, dogs and cats often play in these areas while clothes are hanging on the line drying. In the evenings, adults tend to sit on their verandas and balconies and take advantage of the cooler temperatures. Neighbors chat with each other with the noise of the city (cars, trucks, taxis and dance clubs) as a backdrop. Many walk to the local kiosk to purchase the favorite Cuban ice cream: Coppelia. The youth flock to the local dance clubs to hear a wide variety of music, including rap, salsa, jazz and the more traditional *son* (most contemporary salsa music is based on *son*).

The ethnic makeup of the island is 51 percent mulatto (mix of European and African), 37 percent white, 11 percent black and 1 percent Chinese. The vast majority of its people are Roman Catholic although a large portion of the population practices Afro-Cuban religions. Of these, Santeria, which is a mixture of Catholic and the African Yoruba religious traditions, is the most common. Over the years, Castro, who is an avowed atheist, has come to an accommodation with the Catholic Church and religion in general. In 1991, the Communist Party of Cuba ended its membership prohibition against believers and a year later Cuba was declared a secular rather than an atheist state. This, combined with the historic visit of the pope in 1998, has resulted in many visible signs of religion on the island.

Compared to the vast majority of developing countries in Latin America, Africa and southern Asia, Cuba scores extremely well on virtually all indicators of socioeconomic development: life expectancy, access to healthcare and housing, education levels, employment rates, status of women and infant mortality rates. Its literacy rate of 96 percent compares very favorably with the wealthiest countries in the world. The security net of free healthcare, free education and social security is rarely found among the developing countries of the world. Cuba has an abundance of doctors—approximately 1 for every 200 people. School attendance is mandatory through the ninth grade. The government invests large sums into day care centers and primary, secondary and vocational schools. In 1959, there were only three universities, today, universities are scattered across the entire island. The government provides for a wide variety of cultural and literary programs for all citizens.

THE LAND AND THE ECONOMY

Cuba, covering an area of 44,827 square miles, is the largest island in the Caribbean and is about the size of the state of Pennsylvania. It is located south of Florida, north of Jamaica and to the northwest of Haiti. The island runs approximately 785 miles in an east-west direction and consists mostly of flat to rolling plains with rugged hills and mountains in the southeast. Its temperate tropical climate with adequate rainfall across the island provides an excellent agricultural base for its economy. The rainy season runs from May to October. The soil is also ideally suited for a variety of agricultural crops including sugar cane, tobacco, citrus fruits, coffee, rice, potatoes, beans and livestock. It has deposits of cobalt, nickel, iron ore, copper, manganese, silica and petroleum. The island is estimated to have about 10 percent of the world's known nickel reserves, with most of it found in the highlands on the eastern part of the island. One of the largest single foreign companies on the island is the Canadian company Sherritt with investments in nickel, oil and tourism.

Since colonial days, Cuba has been dependent on trade with the rest of the world in order to survive. Its major industries include sugar, petroleum, food, textiles, tobacco, chemicals, paper and wood products, metals, cement, fertilizers, consumer goods, agricultural machinery and pharmaceuticals. For approximately 150 years, sugar was the dominant industry, but today tourism generates more dollars. Cuban agriculture, which has traditionally been the mainstay of the economy, currently suffers from a lack of foreign exchange (internationally accepted currencies) to purchase sorely needed fertilizers, oil, pesticides and equipment. Most of the island's exports go to Russia, Canada and Spain, while most of its imports are from Spain, Venezuela, France and Canada.

The vast majority of the economic enterprises on the island are run by the state, although private businesses do exist. With the collapse of the Soviet Union in 1991, it was evident that the economy was at a transition point. The island lost about 70 percent of its exports and imports and about $8 billion a year in subsidies and aid. The impact was dramatic. Draconian austerity measures—known as the Special Period—allowed the island to survive the next few years. In order to survive, Cuba needed foreign exchange, capital, technology and markets for its products. The U.S. dollar was legalized in 1993. In 1994, farmers' markets were legalized that enabled the sale of surplus crops for profit. As a result, local food production has increased and food prices have declined. Cuba began courting foreign investors and trading partners. Legal reforms made it easier for foreign companies to invest on the island. Italcable, an Italian firm, is part owner of the island's international telephone service. Free trade zones (FTZs) are located in Havana and Mariel. Goods brought into the FTZs either from within Cuba or from abroad are duty free. Foreign manufacturers that invest on the island receive tax holidays of up to twelve years. There· are more than 290 companies operating in these FTZs. The Cuban government provides highly educated workers for these companies and is able to control the dollars that it so desperately needs. Workers are paid in Cuban pesos. Spain, Italy, Germany, the Netherlands, Austria, Jamaica, Mexico, Martinique, Canada and other countries have investments in the island. Two of the largest investors on the island include Altadis, a Spanish tobacco and cigar distributor, and Stet International, which is a subsidiary of Telecom Intalia.

Large hotel chains, primarily from Spain, Jamaica and Canada have signed joint agreements and are operating in the tourist sectors of the island. Two Cuban companies, Cubanacan and Gaviota, were created to manage the foreign investments in tourism. Both companies are funded in part by the Cuban government and in part by foreign investors. Gaviota is especially known for providing access for foreigners to Cuba's advanced medical technology and eye, open-heart and plastic surgery capabilities. Billboards and wall murals that used to be covered with revolutionary chants now emphasize hospitality and tourism. Varadero, just east of Havana, is the tourist capital of the island with its five-star hotels and beachfront properties that attract hundreds of thousands of tourists from Canada and Europe each year. Those Cubans who are fortunate enough to work in the tourist industry earn much more in dollars than they can at other jobs earning Cuban pesos. It is not uncommon for teachers, engineers and doctors to moonlight as taxi drivers. It is important to note that tourism is a double-edged sword for Castro. It brings in the dollars that the island needs, yet it contributes to a growing economic gap between those Cubans who have access to dollars and those who do not. The egalitarian nature of the revolution is being threatened and resentment among those not in the dollar economy is growing.

The Cuban economy is at a transition point in its history. The primary long-term problem will be its ability to maintain the benefits of the revolution (free healthcare, education and social security) while opening up to the market forces of the global economy. These market forces played a major role in the fall of communism in Eastern Europe and without a doubt they will clearly be Castro's greatest challenge since coming to power in 1959.

THE POLITICAL SYSTEM

Cuba is one of the final bastions of communism in the world today. Castro has ruled the country since 1959. U.S. officials and political pundits have predicted his imminent demise since 1960, yet Castro, the consummate politician, is still very much alive and in charge of the island. He has seen ten U.S. presidents and survived numerous assassination attempts by the U.S. government. There are, however, some noticeable changes. He is older and his beard is much grayer than it used to be. He frequently shows up in a business suit, rather than the army fatigues that have been his traditional signature since his days as a guerrilla commander in the Sierra Maestra mountains of eastern Cuba. He makes fewer public appearances and does not travel around the island nearly

as much as he once did. Still, after more than forty years of revolution, it is the charismatic Castro who will have the most to say
about the future of the island.

There is no freedom of expression as the media are controlled
by the state and Cubans continue to run the risk of imprisonment
if they speak out against the government. Official civic groups
such as the Federation of University Students, the Federation of
Cuban Women and the Union of Young Communists are recognized by the state. Groups must be officially sanctioned by the
state or the members can be jailed. Perhaps the most important
nongovernmental organizations besides the Roman Catholic
Church are the Masons and its female counterpart, the Hijas de
Acacia. Opposition human rights groups such as the Christian
Liberation Movement, the Cuban Commission on Human Rights,
the Cuban Human Rights Committee and the Democratic Solidarity Party do exist but are harassed by the Cuban government.
Outspoken dissidents are held as political prisoners. Perhaps the
most significant dissident movement is the Varela Project, which
is named after Father Felix Varela Morales, a leading intellectual
and nationalist in the early 1800s. This project, organized by Os-
wald Paya of the Christian Liberation Movement, is designed to
collect 10,000 signatures on a petition that will demand a voter
referendum on fundamental rights such as free speech and amnesty for political prisoners. This right to referendum is stated in
Article 88g of the Cuban constitution.

The Communist Party of Cuba is the only legal political party
in the country and it controls the major mass organizations like
the Cuban Workers Central and the National Association of Small
Farmers. Political power at the neighborhood level is vested in the
Committees for the Defense of the Revolution. These elected committees work and help to resolve local problems and issues, but
they also serve a watchdog function over dissident activities. The
degree to which this watchdog function is carried out may vary
considerably from one neighborhood to the next. The Poder Popular (People's Power) are the local legislative assemblies and its
members are elected through direct ballot (since 1993). The People's Power elects members to the provincial assembly and
the provincial assemblies elect members to a national assembly.
The National Assembly is the primary legislative organization.
Non-Communist Party members are free to run for these assemblies and some are elected. The major decision-making bodies are

the Council of Ministers, the Council of State and the Central Committee of the Communist Party of Cuba. Castro is firmly in control of these bodies.

During the Special Period in the early 1990s, the *Miami Herald* reported that Castro was still very popular with most Cubans and that most were very supportive of the three pillars of the revolution: free education, healthcare and social security. Even members of the UN Human Rights Commission, who have been critical of Cuba's violations of human rights, admit that the government has far greater support than what many people outside the country believe. With that said, judging support for Castro is problematic at best. Castro receives much support from those Cubans who lived through the revolution and those who live in the rural areas who have benefited the most from the revolution. Urban workers and the youth are typically more interested in economic gain rather than revolutionary ideals and one should note that more than one-half of all Cubans were born after the revolution. Cubans, even those who are publicly supportive of the revolution, in private are often critical of restrictions on speech and their political activities. Many are tired of the daily struggle and the continued emphasis on building for the future. Yet at the same time, most Cubans have not left the island, even though the guarantee of political asylum if they reach the U.S. mainland is a powerful magnet. Most struggle and continue to work within the revolutionary environment to make a better future for themselves and their children.

The U.S. embargo of the island, which has been in place since 1962, is not supported by the vast majority of countries in the world and has caused some trade disputes between the United States and its Canadian and European allies. Each year since 1992, the UN General Assembly has voted overwhelmingly to condemn the U.S. embargo of the island. Many dissidents within Cuba support an end to the embargo because they say that it gives Castro a scapegoat for his own economic mismanagement. There is no doubt that Castro uses the issue of the embargo very effectively in order to mobilize the Cuban people in support of his policies.

The future of Cuba will be determined by several factors. The first is leadership. There is no doubt that at least in the near future "El Lidér" (Castro) will continue to have the most influence. His charisma, political survival skills and pragmatism—and the fact that Cuba has survived the disastrous economic problems of the

Special Period—have left him firmly in control of the political processes on the island. The other factors that will determine the future of the island are the ongoing relationship with the United States and the effects of the gradual opening of the island to the forces of the world economy. Throughout the remaining pages of this book, it is argued that these factors have always determined the future of the island. For Castro one could substitute Fulgencio Batista, Gerardo Machado or other leaders who have controlled the country at one time or another. All Cuban leaders have had to learn to deal with and react to a powerful, hegemonic country whether it was colonial Spain or the United States. Finally, the Cuban economy has always been dependent on or vulnerable to world economic forces. Since the 1860s, the fluctuations in the world market price of sugar have directly affected the success and failure of the economy. These are the constants in Cuban history and it is the interplay of these constants that have determined the past—and will determine the future—of the island.

2

Early Cuba: Colonialism, Sugar and Nationalism: Cuba to 1868

It is quite common today to hear people talk about how events in one part of the world have a direct impact on other parts of the world. People and media commentators often speak of global interdependence as if it were something new. Yet, during the four centuries of Spanish rule over Cuba (1492–1898) one can easily see how events in the Caribbean, Spain, greater Europe and the United States directly affected the island. One can also see how events in Cuba directly affected the world beyond its borders. It is not insignificant that one of the primary consequences or legacies of Spanish colonialism is that the island became part of an interdependent world never fully in control of its own destiny.

The indigenous peoples of Cuba were either wiped out through disease and Spanish brutality or absorbed through intermarriage in the late 1400s and 1500s. They would not play a significant role in the development of Cuba. The *conquistadores*, after discovering the island did not have significant deposits of gold and silver, quickly moved on to the immense wealth and treasures found in the Aztec and Inca empires in what is today Mexico and Peru. Thus, for nearly 300 years the island of Cuba was relegated to serving merely as a stopping over point between Spain and the riches from its colonies in Spanish America (Mexico and Central and South America). Little change would take place until several events in the late 1700s set the stage for the island's transformation. These included an eleven-month occupation of Havana by the English in 1762, the emergence of the United States as a market for Cuba, the Spanish Crown's liberalizing trade reforms of 1778 and 1791, and, perhaps most importantly, a slave rebellion in St. Domingue (Haiti) in 1791 that dramatically affected the world market for sugar. These events set into motion forces that would radically alter the destiny of the island.

With St. Domingue no longer producing sugar, the world market price increased. Increases in sugar production with growing demand in the United States and Europe brought tremendous wealth to the emerging Cuban Creole (Spaniards born in the New World) planter class (large landowners). As the sugar trade expanded dramatically, the United States became the major market for Cuban sugar by the middle of the 1800s. In fact, noted historian Louis A. Pérez Jr. points out that by that time North America had come to replace Spain as a point of reference for most Cubans, the United States had come to represent progress and modernization and Spain, decline and backwardness.

At the same time, there were negative consequences to the sugar boom. It exacerbated the economic inequality on the island. Most did not share in the newfound wealth. Sugar escalated the island's dependence on the slave trade, although ironically this occurred when many countries were banning it and, in fact, Spain agreed to suppress the slave trade in 1817. Of course, it continued and prospered illegally. This also occurred at a time when abolitionist groups were challenging the very institution of slavery. Slave rebellions were common throughout the first six decades of the 1800s. The island's wealthy Creoles came into sharp conflict with the *peninsulares* (Spaniards living in the New World who were born in Spain) over restrictive trade policies and the lack of opportunity to participate in the political decision-making processes. But Cuban nationalism would be hindered by the lack of agreement over the issue of slavery. This divided the nationalist movement and made the struggle for Cuba Libre (independence) in the second half of the 1800s most difficult.

PRECOLONIAL AND COLONIAL CUBA

When Christopher Columbus arrived in Cuba in 1492, there were three different indigenous peoples on the island: the Tainos, the Ciboneys and the Guanajatabeyes. The best estimates are that there were between 50,000 and 300,000 indigenous peoples at the time. In the next seventy years, most of the indigenous peoples on the island were killed largely due to Spanish cruelty and diseases such as smallpox, typhus, influenza and measles. Others intermarried and a few Indian villages such as El Cobre (near Santiago), Guanabacoa (near Havana) and Pueblo Viejo (near Bayamo) still exist. The cave-dwelling Guanajatabeyes were the first indigenous peoples on the island and the smallest in numbers. They were fruit and food gatherers and lived primarily on a diet of sea mollusks. They lived on the western part of the island and rarely came in contact with the Spanish. The Ciboneys were part of the Arawak group from South America that spread throughout the West Indies. They fished, hunted and practiced some agriculture. The Ciboneys became servants to the more advanced Tainos. The largest indigenous group was the Tainos, who arrived in Cuba in the 1400s from the West Indies. They slept in hammocks, fished, hunted and grew fruits, beans, peanuts, corn, and their staple food manioc (yucca). They carved furniture, weaved cotton, baked cassava (a hearty, unleavened bread that the Spanish called "bread of the earth") and used pepper to preserve meat. Tobacco and snuff were used in religious ceremonies and they lived in straw, palm-thatched houses called *bohios*. The Tainos had three distinct social classes: the chiefs (*caciques*), a small middle class that acted as advisers to the chiefs, and commoners. Although many Indian words made their way into the Spanish language that is used on the island, the indigenous peoples had little impact on Cuban political, economic and social development. Until the middle of the nineteenth century, Cuban cultural identity was shaped primarily by Spanish colonialism, the importation of African slaves and an economy based on sugar.

Spanish colonialism in the New World was fueled by the missionary zeal to convert non-Christians, the Crown's desire for gold and silver and the personal motives of the *conquistadores* and settlers. In the late 1400s and early 1500s, Spanish power in the Caribbean was located on the island of Hispaniola. The island lacked a reliable labor force and, more importantly, it lacked the gold and silver that Spain wanted. Believing that Cuba had plenty of gold, Sebastian de Ocampo explored and sailed around the island in 1508. In 1511, Diego Velázquez landed near Baracoa and established the first Spanish settlement. He served as the first governor until his death in 1524. The indigenous peoples in the eastern part of the island fought Velázquez and the conquerors but were defeated largely due to the superior weapons of the Spanish. A small amount of gold was found in Cuba and the indigenous peoples worked the mines at La Mina (close to Havana) and near Bayamo. Others were forced to pan for gold in the Arimao, Escambray and Holquin Rivers. Velázquez issued *encomiendas* as a method of controlling the Indians. The *encomienda* system legally tied the indigenous peoples to Spaniards. The indigenous peoples served as laborers and, in return, were converted and given instruction in Christianity. Cruelty, physical abuse and overwork were common practices by the Spanish *encomenderos*. The indigenous population of Cuba was so small by 1513 that the first Africans were imported as slave laborers.

It was from Cuba that Hernán Cortés left for Mexico in 1519. Santiago de Cuba with its excellent harbor had been settled four years earlier and was the most important city on the island. By the middle of the century, the focus of Spanish power shifted from the Caribbean to Mexico and South America largely due to the vast amounts of gold and silver found there and the realization that there was little to be found in Cuba. Many on the island left for Mexico and South America with the *conquistadores* in search of fortune and fame. For many years, the population on the island declined. Day-to-day life was extremely difficult and uncertain with the genuine fear of slave uprisings and attack by the English or the French. By 1544, there were no more than 7,000 people on the island and of these 660 were Spanish, 800 were slaves and the remainder were indigenous peoples.[1] The Catholic Church provided the only education.

It was at this time that Havana with its deep-water harbor became the most important city on the island. It had become the "key to the New World." It served as a transition point for the riches taken from the Americas that were going to Spain because ships could take advantage of the Gulf Stream that helped to carry them eastward and the shifting trade winds between winter and summer. For about a month of each year, the Spanish fleet waited in Havana for the treasure ships coming from Mexico and Central and South America. The fleet then escorted them to Cádiz or Seville. As a result, Havana became a military and shipbuilding center, a provider of supplies (salt beef, leather, vegetables and fruit) for the fleet's return trip to Spain and a naval seaport. La Fuerza, the first military fortress made of stone in the New World, was built in Havana between 1558 and 1577. Shipbuilding became one of the major industries in the late 1500s. By 1592, the city had constructed a canal that brought fresh water from the Almendares River. According to scholars Roberto Segre, Mario Coyula and Joseph Scarpaci, this was the first public works program in the New World and it was funded primarily from taxes on the sale of wine. Two other fortresses were completed by 1610.

The vast wealth and riches of Mexico and South America bypassed Cuba, so the island and its inhabitants turned to their primary resource: land. The large forests of mahogany and cedar supported the growing shipbuilding industry in Havana. Mahogany was also exported to Spain to meet the needs of the furniture industry. Spaniards received land grants called *mercedes* from which they were to meet the beef needs of both the neighboring towns and the Spanish fleet. Sweet potatoes, yams, corn, beans and yucca were cultivated as well. Sugar cane was introduced as early as the second voyage of Columbus and there were a few mills (*trapiches*) founded in the 1520s. But sugar would not become important to Cuba for another two centuries largely due to the nonavailability of credit, the low demand in Spain and the expense of providing an adequate labor supply. Large cattle ranches covered much of Cuba and leather and hides were the largest exports until the early 1700s. Tobacco was initially grown in areas that had easy access to port facilities such as in Havana and Trinidad. Snuff was particularly sought after by the smugglers. It is important to note that under Spanish mercantilism practices, those on the island could legally only trade with Spain. This made it difficult to gain access to European goods at the cheapest prices. Even though the French, English and Dutch were maritime and political rivals of Spain and encouraged piracy against the Spanish, merchants in Cuba engaged in some profitable illegal trade with them largely because they offered goods at a lower price than what could be obtained from Seville. It was this desire for access to cheaper goods that began to create a conflict of interest between the Spanish Crown and its settlers in Cuba.

The colonial governing structure in Cuba was headed by a governor who was appointed by the Crown. Initially, the local governing institution of each settlement—the *cabilido*—was given significant autonomy. Members of the local *cabilido* elected a *procurador* who met annually with other *procuradores* in Santiago. These individuals discussed local grievances and issues of importance to their settlement and the island as a whole. This group elected a representative to present these issues and grievances to the governor, the Crown's representative. This practice came to an end in 1532 as the governors sought to centralize the political processes in the Spanish colonies in the New World. The Crown's administrative control over Cuba and the rest of its New World colonies came to reside with the *peninsulares.* Local administrative positions were sold by the Crown at auction. Corruption and patronage became common practice. Creoles rarely achieved political positions of high rank. Over time, this inability of Creoles to participate in the decision-making processes created a growing resentment toward the *peninsulares* that manifested itself in the growth of nationalism and the desire for independence in the second half of the nineteenth century.

From the middle of the 1500s and throughout the 1600s, England, France and the Netherlands competed with Spain for control of the Caribbean. Spanish cities were under constant threat of attack and its treasure fleets were prime targets. By the early 1600s, the English, Dutch and French were also actively seeking new colonies in the region. With the English capture of Jamaica in 1655, the Spaniards in Cuba became quite concerned over the probability of attack. The European countries created their own buccaneers (mercenaries who engaged in piracy during nonwar periods) and attacked each other's settlements and colonies. Cuba was brutalized by the English buccaneer Henry Morgan, who attacked the eastern part of the island and terrorized its settlers. Spanish buccaneers frequently attacked Jamaica (England) and St. Domingue (France). Recognizing the loss in potential revenues due to these attacks, the English and Spanish sought to end hostilities and trade peacefully. In 1670, Spain recognized England's colonies in the Caribbean and in 1697 France agreed to end its buccaneer raids in the Caribbean in exchange for recognition of its authority over St. Domingue (Haiti).

By the early 1700s, tobacco had replaced leather and hides as the dominant economic sector of Cuba largely due to growing demand in Europe. Tobacco farms (*vegas*) were located throughout the island but primarily in the western part (Pinar del Río) along the Cuyaguateje River, where the best tobaccos are grown. The Spanish created an official monopoly on tobacco in 1717. Local producers had to sell their product to the Crown's purchasing agency (*estanco*) either in Havana or other major cities where it was then sold to Cádiz or Seville. There were protests and even rebellions against these trade restrictions that were met with repression by the Crown. Despite the restrictions, a local cottage industry flourished and much of the tobacco crop and snuff went to smugglers from other countries.

In 1713, the South Sea Company of London was granted both limited trading rights with and an exclusive license (*asiento*) to sell slaves to the Spanish colonies until 1739. A Spanish company was granted a monopoly on the sale of slaves after that, although the company bought the slaves from the South Sea Company. Even with the smuggling of slaves into the island, Creole planters simply could not get enough slaves and this contributed to the limitations on the growth of the sugar industry. They preferred male rather than female slaves to work in the cane fields and believed that regularly replacing slaves through the importation of new ones was cheaper than raising slave children. Females were also seen as less productive and more costly should they become pregnant. This meant that Cuban planters had to depend on a continual replenishment of the supply of slaves. Another problem was that only a few of the wealthy, established Creole families could afford to purchase slaves. Also, much of the land that was converted to the production of sugar in the middle of the 1700s took place on established estates by the wealthiest Creole families. Others converted tobacco lands to sugar when the tobacco state monopoly was created and some converted parts of their cattle ranches. Since there was no banking system in Cuba, the Creole planters often borrowed from local merchants at exorbitant interest rates. In fact, from 1740 to 1760 more than 80 percent of the slaves in Cuba were purchased on credit.[2] Planters were, in more ways than one, dependent on the merchants not only for loans, but also for everything else, from wine and wheat to imported machinery and tools.

The cattle ranchers, the tobacco and sugar planters and the merchants in the urban areas were at the top of Cuban society during the eighteenth century. Beneath them were small landowners, usually tobacco growers, lawyers and skilled tradesmen such as carpenters and individuals who managed the large plantations of the Creole planters. Below this group existed a large number of people (Europeans, mulattos and freed slaves) who worked for wages and lacked the resources to ever own land. Finally, at the bottom of the class structure were the slaves who worked primarily on the sugar plantations. By 1774, the population of Cuba had reached 170,000 of which about 40 percent were mulatto or African. Havana, a walled and heavily fortified city, had a permanent garrison of Spanish soldiers and a population of about 75,000. It had a large population of free mulattos and Africans estimated to be about 10,000.[3]

SETTING THE STAGE FOR THE RISE OF KING SUGAR

Several events in the late 1700s and early 1800s set the stage for the growth of the sugar industry on the island. Spain allied with France in its struggle with the English during the Seven Years War (1756–1763). In August 1762, the English under Lord Albemarle attacked and occupied Havana. Juan de Prado, the island's governor and captain-general, the Spanish administrators and virtually all the *peninsulares* left the island. The English eliminated the Spanish trade restrictions and more than 700 merchant ships visited Havana during the occupation.[4] This opened Havana to a large number of goods from North America and England. Grain and slave merchants and dealers in sugar equipment such as machetes, cauldrons and ladles arrived. Items such as horses, hats, stockings, linen, cloth and wool were available. Eleven months later, the English traded Cuba back to Spain in exchange for Florida in the Treaty of Paris that ended the war. This was largely due to the lobbying influence of the English sugar planters in Jamaica who prophetically saw Cuban sugar as a future competitor. But the impact of these eleven months would be felt throughout the island. The Cuban Creoles had received their first taste of free trade and they liked it. They also became aware of the potential of investment from North Americans, the large North American market for their goods and access to new technology. The Creole sugar planters benefited immediately from the English occupation largely due to the increased availability of slave labor and equipment. Sugar production increased almost overnight. Sugar exports prior to the English occupation had averaged 300 tons a year and from 1763 through 1769 they averaged 2,000 tons a year.[5]

Conde de Ricla, the new Spanish governor and captain-general, had Havana strengthened by building another fort, La Cabana. This construction required a large increase in the number of slaves and when construction was completed most of them were sold on the market to sugar planters. By 1774, there were more than 44,000 slaves in Cuba.[6] With the Spanish treasure fleets no longer regularly coming to Havana, much of the shipping industry was converted to build cauldrons and ladles for sugar mills. Sugar exports reached 10,000 tons a year during the 1770s.[7] In 1778, the Bourbon monarch Charles III of Spain, in an effort to revive the empire's economic growth, issued his Decree of Free Trade that allowed the twenty-four ports in Spanish America to trade freely among themselves and with any port in Spain. By 1790, sugar production had reached 14,000 tons.[8] In 1791, Charles III agreed to allow the free and unlimited importation of slaves largely due to the lobbying efforts of Cuban Creole planter Francisco de Arrongo. By the next year, the number of slaves on the island reached more than 84,000.[9] When the war between Spain and France started the following year, Arrongo and other Creole planters convinced Captain-General Don Luis de las Casas (who also owned a sugar plantation) that Cuban ports should be open to neutral and allied shipping—in particular, the United States and England.

In 1791, a slave rebellion started in the French colony of St. Domingue. St. Domingue was the largest producer of sugar in the world at the time. By the time the slaves, who were led by Toussaint-Louverture and Jean-Jacques Dessalines, had won their independence in 1804, more than 180 sugar and 900 coffee plantations had been destroyed. More than 2,000 Europeans and 10,000 African slaves had lost their lives. Sugar exports declined from 70,000 tons in 1791 to 2,020 in 1825.[10] This created a tremendous opportunity for the expansion of the Cuban sugar industry. Many of the French planters fled to Cuba and brought with them their sugar expertise to areas around Cienfuegos, Nipe, Banes and Nuevitas. By 1796, the price of sugar had almost doubled and England provided one-third of the island's imports and purchased one-half of its exports. At the same time, Cuba began turning more and more to the United States for its exports and imports. In the same year, only 100 U.S. ships arrived in Cuba, yet by 1800 that had increased to 606 ships. By 1805, there were twice as many sugar mills in Cuba as there were before the English occupation of Havana and sugar production reached 34,000 tons.[11]

Arrongo, Conde de Casa Montalvo, Jose Ricardo O'Farrill and other modernizing Creoles were intent on creating a rich, sugar-based economy in Cuba. It was to be based on the expansion of slavery, better infrastructure, modern sugar mills (*ingenios*) and greater access to capital or finances and the world market. They helped create Cuba's first newspaper and came to represent a Cuban nationalist rather than a Spanish point of view. This reform-minded and nationalist viewpoint manifested itself in the creation of the Economic Society (Sociedad Economia de Amigos del Pais). The members of the society were well educated, urban and inter-nationalist in their orientation. They played a primary role in developing an intellectual climate with the support of Creole planters that resulted in dramatic changes to Cuban economic policies in the early 1800s. In particular, the Economic Society was responsible for the land reform that set the stage for the growth of the sugar industry. Land that was previously held in usufruct (a condition in which a person did not own the land but could profit from the crops grown on the land) became private property as long as the person could show he had been in possession of the land for ninety years and had been cultivating it for forty years. Cattle ranchers holding *mercedes* were no longer required to provide beef for the neighboring cities and could manage their lands as they saw fit. Fighting a war against France and needing to replenish its treasury, the Crown agreed to begin to sell its land to Cuban Creoles. Trees, especially hardwood forests of mahogany, could now be cleared for agricultural production. These reforms increased the number of landowners and allowed property owners greater freedom in the use of the land.

The sugar boom in the aftermath of the slave rebellion in St. Domingue came to an end just after the turn of the century. With high prices during the 1790s, sugar production increased throughout the Caribbean and in Europe where the sugar beet had been introduced. This created a sugar surplus on the world market and drove the price down. Other factors also made it difficult for the growth of the sugar industry during the first two decades of the century. These included the wars of independence in Spanish America, the campaign to end the slave trade and the growth of the coffee industry. By 1808, Napoléon Bonaparte occupied the Iberian Peninsula and placed his brother Joseph on the Spanish Crown. This event was the catalyst for the wars of independence in the Spanish colonies in the Americas that lasted from 1810 through the mid-1820s. But, the Creole planter class in Cuba remained "ever faithful" to the Crown and did not join this struggle for several reasons. Large numbers of Spanish troops who were involved in the fight against the revolutionaries were stationed in Cuba. It would have been most difficult to defeat these troops. The growing wealth from tobacco, coffee and sugar and greater control over the use of their own land led the Creole planters to believe that the risk and cost of failure was too great. Finally, the memory of the tremendous destruction during the slave rebellion in Haiti also weighed on their decision because by this time there were more Africans (slaves and free) than Europeans on the island.

In 1808, Denmark, England and the United States banned the slave trade. Sweden, France and Holland quickly followed. This abolitionist movement was clearly a threat to the future of the island in the eyes of the Creole planters. Arrongo and other Cuban Creoles extensively lobbied the Spanish government not to abolish the slave trade. Nonetheless, Spain, under tremendous pressure from powerful England, who played the dominant role in the coalition that defeated Napoléon, agreed to end the slave trade by 1820. In reaction to this, Cuba imported more than 100,000 slaves from 1816 to 1820—as many or more than were imported in the previous 300 years.[12] Creole planters encouraged the governor to "turn a blind eye" to the ban and it was common practice for illegal slave traders regularly to pay tribute or bribes to the governors and captain-generals in Cuba after 1820.

During the first two decades of the century, the price of coffee remained high and many coffee planters saw no reason to plant sugar cane. Coffee plantations (*cafetales*) were largely the result of the French exodus from St. Domingue. The best coffee growing regions were in Pinar del Río, the area southwest of Havana and the region around Santiago. By 1827, Cuba was exporting 20,000 tons of coffee and there was more land devoted to the production of coffee than sugar.[13] Yet, many of these planters also owned sugar estates and, according to noted historian Hugh Thomas, by 1829 they realized that the return on their investment in coffee was less than the return on their investment in sugar. Coffee production in Cuba declined until 1834 and then remained constant until the mid-1840s. Production then declined precipitously largely due to growing competition from Brazil. More and more *cafetales* were converted to the production of sugar cane. Coffee would continue to be grown on the island but the stage was set for the dominance of sugar. It is important to note that coffee planters on the eastern part of the island came to blame sugar for the decline of their fortunes. They came to see the sugar industry, sugar planters, slavery and the Spanish Crown in the same negative light. Some of them would initiate the independence movement in the 1860s.

With the Crown's monopoly on tobacco ending in 1817, it also continued to be a major product of Cuba. By the middle of the century, Cuban cigars were in great demand in Europe and the United States. By this time, as they are now, they were considered to be the best in the world. In 1860, there were 11,500 *vegas* on the island with 130 cigar factories in Havana.[14] But tobacco was never a large user of slave labor and typically the work on the *vegas* was done by either free men or the family of the owner. According to Thomas, *vegas* were usually no more than thirty-three acres in size with plantains and vegetables being grown on half the land. Thus, tobacco never competed with the growth of sugar on the island.

THE RISE OF KING SUGAR

By 1818, Cuban ports were opened to all nations of the world and a small number of sugar planters installed steam engines at their mills. Increasingly, the planters turned to North America for their necessary technology and capital and for a market for their sugar. Modernization was necessary in order for Cuban cane sugar to compete with European beet sugar. Steam engines arrived from Merrick and Sons of Philadelphia, Novelty Iron Works in New York and Isaac and Seth Porter of Boston. American engineers and technicians arrived regularly to operate and maintain them during the harvest season. New technology and investment funds from the United States began to transform the sugar industry and Cuba's trade relationships. Cuba became more and more oriented toward the United States.

During the first part of century, the increase in sugar production was achieved largely through the growth in the number of mills rather than an increase in the size of the mills and plantations. Sugar plantations remained small, largely due to the lack of roads and railroads to get the cane from the fields to the mills. It should be noted that after the cane is cut it must reach the mill within two days or the fermentation process begins. The trees around the mills were used as fuel and it was difficult to transport wood over long distances. Thus, the lack of adequate infrastructure led to an increase in the number of mills and plantations rather than an increase in their size in the early 1800s. By 1827 there were 1,000 mills across the island.

The sugar wealth exploded after 1830 with the growth of the railroads (imported from the United States) through the important sugar growing areas of Matanzas to Union de Reyes, Puerto-Principe to Nuevitas, Cienfuegos to Santa Clara, Cárdenas to Colón, Remedios to Caibarien, Matanzas to Jovellanos, Casilda to Trinidad and Havana to Matanzas. Havana was linked to New York, Philadelphia, Baltimore, Mobile, New Orleans and Key West via regular steamship service by 1836 and by 1850 there were more than 600 miles of railroad linking the sugar areas to Havana and the major port cities.[15] The wealth derived from the tax revenues from sugar was easily visible in Havana. In the 1830s, Governor Miguel Tacon engaged in public works programs that paved many of the roads, installed public lighting, built a theater house, created wide boulevards with trees on each side, installed sewer lines, repaired the port facilities, dredged the harbor and constructed a train station. The captain-general's palace in the Plaza de Armas was remodeled. In 1837, a passenger service railroad line was established between Havana and Bejucal.

In addition to engineers and machine operators, U.S. retailers, shipping agents and freight handlers began to appear in Cuba, primarily in Havana and the other port cities. They provided manufactured goods, foodstuffs and insurance. Merchants extended credit to sugar planters. This was often done in exchange for sugar and molasses that were then exported to the United States. Some Americans owned and operated sugar estates. Others were responsible for developing the telegraph service both within Cuba and between Havana and Key West.

Due to the growth of sugar technology, the arrival of railroads and other infrastructure improvements and competition from the rest of the Caribbean and sugar beet producers in Europe, Cuban planters began building larger sugar mills (*centrales*). Modern, large mills could process more sugar but they required more fuel and employees. The need for more cane for their mills led the *centrales* either to acquire their own cane fields or to assume greater control over the tenants (*colonos*). Some of the owners of the *centrales* were owners of large sugar plantations, others were not. Typically, the land on these plantations was cultivated either by resident laborers (slaves) or by *colonos* who worked the land for a salary or for a share of the crop. By 1860, there were 2,000 sugar mills on the island and Cuba was producing one-third of the world's sugar.

One could identify three different groups of sugar planters by the middle of the century. The first were the old oligarchs such as the Cardenas, Alfonsos, Betancourt, O'Farrill, Iznagas, Arangos, Calvos and Herreras families, whose ancestors had bought their land prior to the nineteenth century. The second group included self-made immigrants, mostly from Spain. They typically were merchants before becoming planters and usually had more technologically advanced mills than the oligarchs. Tomás Terry who came from Venezuela and settled in Cienfuegos was the first planter in Cuba to use electricity at his mill Caracas. A third group of sugar planters consisted of estates that were owned by companies such as the Noreiga Olmo and Company of Havana and Barcelona. The sugar planters often built opulent mansions, although many actually lived in their homes in Havana, Santiago or Matanzas and only visited the plantations during the sugar harvest. The plantations were typically run by an administrator who may or may not have been a member of the planter family. The homes frequently had marble fountains, baths and large staircases. Planters often bought titles of rank such as count, marques or gentleman from the Crown, which accorded them a certain social status and rights such as the protection from arrest for debt. It was almost a competition among the planters as to who could adorn their carriages with the most jewelry, silver and gold. They spent much money on entertainment, especially masked or costume balls and dances. Cockfighting and bullfighting were other favorite pastimes of the planters. Many invested their wealth in the United States and Europe and continued to engage in the illegal slave trade. The great irony of the wealth of the sugar planters in Cuba is that many were heavily in debt to merchants since the first bank did not appear on the island until after the middle of the century. Of course, this immense sugar wealth was built on the institution of slavery with virtually all of the largest sugar plantations using slaves for the backbreaking work of cutting cane.

THE ISSUE OF SLAVERY

It is estimated that most of the approximate 400,000 slaves imported illegally into Cuba after 1820 worked on plantations producing sugar, molasses and rum. The remainder worked on coffee estates, cattle ranches and in the city. Many in the city were able to earn enough money to purchase their freedom and the large nonslave African population was involved in trades such as driving the carriages (*volantes*) of the wealthy planters, carpentering, tailoring, laundering, shoe making and cigar making. By 1861, Hugh Thomas estimates that freed slaves and mulattoes represented 16 percent of the population.

For the sugar planters, slaves represented the largest single investment. The high price of the slaves even offset the money-saving technological advances, such as steam engines and vacuum boilers, that came to be seen on the larger plantations by the middle of the 1850s. Plantation slaves worked under desperate conditions especially during the five to six months of sugar harvest. Twenty-hour workdays were the norm. Many died from overwork, accidents or sickness. On the large plantations, most slaves were typically housed in large barracks. The only form of entertainment was dancing. Drum dances held on Sundays or during fiestas were frequently attended by the planters and the plantation overseers. African religions mixed with the official religion of Catholicism. Slaves developed their own folklore that reflected their lives in Africa and Cuba.

There was a constant fear among the sugar planters that either Great Britain or a weak Spanish government being pressured by Great Britain could force them to live up to the treaty obligations of 1820 and free all the slaves imported illegally. They also lived in constant fear of slave uprisings and most had long memories of the Haitian revolution. Major slave rebellions occurred in 1826, 1837, 1843 and 1844. The uprising in Matanzas in 1844 resulted in 4,000 arrests, including freed slaves and mulattoes and at least 70 Creoles. Seventy-eight conspirators were shot and more than 100 were whipped to death by local authorities.[16] Cuban planters, mostly those of the Club de la Habana, turned to the United States, especially the southern slave states. Some were hopeful of a permanent relationship that would protect the institution of slavery on the island. They were convinced that the Spanish government was going to give in to English pressure to free all the slaves imported illegally into Cuba. Proslavery groups in the southern United States saw the annexation of Cuba as a way of increasing their power within the Congress. Others in the United States supported annexation based on claims of manifest destiny. President James Polk even tried to purchase the island. Some of these groups, both within the United States and Cuba, encouraged armed expeditions (called filibusters) with the hope of overthrowing Spanish control on the island. All of these filibusters, the most famous led by Narciso Lopez in 1850 and 1851, ended in failure. The U.S. Civil War ended the talk of annexation as Cuban planters were forced to depend solely on the Spanish Crown to continue to protect the institution of slavery and to overlook the illegal slave trade. Many came to see that the illegal slave trade was coming to an end and that Cuba would not be able to replenish its slave labor. Without the ability to replenish its slave labor, they believed that the institution of slavery would eventually die out for economic reasons.

The U.S. Civil War also destroyed the sugar plantations in Louisiana and paved the way for an expansion of Cuban sugar production in the 1860s. By this time, advances in technology were making the larger sugar plantations more efficient in the refining of sugar and creating an economic disincentive in the use of costly slave labor. Of course, only the largest plantations could afford slaves and new technologies. Small sugar plantations could afford neither the technology nor the necessary number of slaves to produce sugar at a competitive price. By 1865, the first actual slave strike occurred. Slaves demanded payment for their work and peacefully asserted their right to freedom because they had arrived in Cuba after 1820. Troops ended the strike but this was a clear indication of the growing difficulty of using slave labor for Cuba's main export. Finally, an increase in Asian immigrants increased the pool of wage laborers available to plantation owners who were willing to experiment in nonslave labor. This was especially true in Oriente, in eastern Cuba, where the smaller, poorer and less modern sugar planters had experimented with wage laborers. Some had already freed their slaves and then hired them as wage laborers. Some, seeing their economic fortunes decline compared to the modern plantations of central Cuba, saw rebellion as an option.

THE GROWTH OF NATIONALISM

Cuban Creoles remained loyal to the Crown during the wars of independence and the growth of sugar wealth early in the century retarded the growth of nationalism among the sugar planters. Yet, Creole elites were becoming increasingly dissatisfied with the trade limitations and restrictions associated with its colonial status, the lack of a real voice in the political processes on the island and the corruption of the local government officials. As discussed earlier, the Economic Society was the first institution to become a voice of Cuban nationalism and its members successfully pressured the Spanish government for several economic reforms. Bishop Diaz de Espada, one of the founders of the society, liberalized the curriculum at the Real Colegio Seminario de San Carlos in Havana and it served as a breeding ground for soon-to-be prominent Cuban Creole intellectuals such as Felix Varela and Jose Antonio Saco. By the 1830s, Cuban poets such as Jose Maria Herdia, Juan Clemente Zenea, Hernandez Echerri and Miguel Teurbe Tolon became the voices of those desiring independence from Spain. Some Cuban planters, as discussed earlier, promoted annexation to the United States as an alternative to Spanish colonialism. Others, such as Saco, questioned the development of a closer relationship with the United States. They came to fear U.S. dominance as much as Spanish dominance. Other groups came to support reform within the existing colonial relationship. Reform rather than rebellion was preferred by many planters because the Crown was still the best protection for the institution of slavery on the island.

In an effort to sway a growing nationalist movement, the administrations of Captain-General Francisco Serrano (1859–1962) and Domingo Dulce (1862–1865) were more tolerant of Cuban Creole demands. Proposed political reforms were published in *El Siglo* and Serrano even proposed that Cuban Creoles be given the right to participate in the Spanish Cortes. The reform movement in Cuba reached a peak in 1865 with the creation of the Reform Party, which wanted Cuban Creoles to have the same political rights as the *peninsulares*, greater economic freedom and limits on the power of the captain-general. *Peninsulares* formed their own party, the Unconditional Spanish Party, to counter the demands of the reformists. Spain, in an attempt to moderate some of the demands, then called for the election of a reform commission that was charged with the task of discussing the political and economic needs and reforms on the island within the colonial framework. The reform commission, which consisted of no less than twelve Creole reformers, adopted several reforms in late 1866 and early 1867, including representation in the Spanish Cortes, freedom from arbitrary arrests and the requirement that Creoles be given equal access to government positions.[17] The commission called for the gradual end to slavery.

Hope for reform was quickly ended as a new, reactionary government in Spain disbanded the commission and refused to implement the proposed reforms. It also appointed Francisco Lersundi as the new captain-general of Cuba. Lersundi asserted an iron-fisted rule by censoring the local press and clamping down on all forms of political activity. It was clear to many that reform was not possible and the stage was set for a violent struggle for independence. It would begin in the east near Bayamo and be led by Carlos Manuel de Céspedes, the patriarch of a sugar planter family that traced its roots in Cuba to 1517.

CUBA AT THE BRINK OF THE WARS FOR INDEPENDENCE

By 1861, the population of Cuba had reached 1.4 million people of which 30 percent were African or of African descent. There were 10 cities that had a population in excess of 10,000, including the large port cities of Havana and Santiago. With the original city walls coming down in the early 1860s, the growth of elite neighborhoods and a thriving commercial and port center, Havana was a metropolis of more than 390,000 people. Tourism in Havana was a growing industry with an estimated 5,000 U.S. vacationers arriving annually by 1860.[18] The number of North American ships arriving in Cuban ports increased annually from 529 in 1792 to more than 2,088 between 1851 and 1856. By 1850, more than one-half of Cuba's sugar was exported to the United States. Foreign trade, most of it passing through Havana, amounted to more than $92 million by 1862.[19] Sugar production reached more than 500,000 tons between 1862 and 1864 and more than 600,000 tons by 1867. It was the largest producer of sugar in the world. Cuba's wealthy planter class stood in dramatic contrast with the majority of Cubans who did not benefit from sugar wealth. This was easily seen in Havana with its new elite neighborhoods and large numbers of poor immigrants, Creoles, mulattos and freed slaves who survived on diets of plantain, jerked beef, fish, tobacco, cheap Spanish wine and *guarapo* (cane juice). Begging and prostitution were common. Shantytowns on the outskirts of the city continued to expand. In sum, Cuba's economic growth during the first half of the century was impressive by any measure. The increase in sugar production, the greater use of technology, the development of the infrastructure on the island, the growth in tourism, the rise of Havana as a major world trading center and the growth in trade with other countries clearly indicated tremendous progress. Yet, at the same time it is also important to point out that the benefits of that growth and progress were clearly not shared very evenly among its population. In particular, the slave population of Cuba continued to suffer.

By 1868, many Cuban elites had come to the conclusion that only a break with Spain would give them the political and economic freedoms they so desperately sought. In the countryside, a restless and more assertive slave population could form the basis of an army that could be mobilized against its Spanish colonial masters. At the same time, it served as a threat to the economic well-being of wealthy planters who continued to defend the use of slaves in the production of sugar. This double-edged sword would play a major role in Cuba's first attempt to win its independence from Spain from 1868 to 1878.

NOTES

1. Jaime Suchlicki, *Cuba: From Columbus to Castro,* 2nd ed. (Washington, D.C.: Pergamon-Brassey's, 1986), 28.

2. Hugh Thomas, *Cuba; the Pursuit of Freedom* (New York: Harper and Row, 1971), 33.

3. Ibid., 65.

4. Ibid., 51.

5. Ibid., 61.

6. Ibid., 65.

7. Ibid., 61.

8. Suchlicki, *Cuba,* 45.

9. Thomas, *Cuba; the Pursuit of Freedom,* 92.

10. Ibid., 76, 77.

11. Suchlicki, *Cuba,* 45.

12. Thomas, *Cuba; the Pursuit of Freedom,* 95.

13. Ibid., 129.

14. Ibid., 134.

15. Louis A. Pérez Jr., *On Becoming Cuban* (Chapel Hill: University of North Carolina Press, 1999), 18.

16. Thomas, *Cuba; the Pursuit of Freedom*, 205.

17. Suchlicki, *Cuba*, 63.

18. Pérez, *On Becoming Cuban*, 23.

19. Louis A. Pérez Jr., *Slaves, Sugar, and Colonial Society* (Wilmington, Del.: Scholarly Resources, 1992), xvii.

3

The Wars for Independence and U.S. Occupation: 1868 to 1902

Wars for independence are often precipitated by the desire of economic and political elites to have greater control over their own destinies. These wars are typically associated with the growth of nationalism and they tend to create heroes that are venerated by subsequent generations. Wars for independence also often come with unanticipated consequences. All of these characteristics fit Cuba Libre, the Cuban struggle for independence from Spain. The growth of a Cuban identity and nationalism was tied to the desire of the island's economic elites to have more control over their own political and economic futures. The struggle created national heroes such as Carlos Manuel de Céspedes, Antonio Maceo (the Bronze Titan) and the father figure of modern Cuba: José Martí. The tremendous damage done to the economic infrastructure and the elimination of the island's primary economic elites—the Creole sugar oligarchy (aristocratic landowning class)—had the unanticipated outcome of making it possible for a more than willing and opportunistic United States to expand its economic presence and, ultimately, its political and cultural dominance over the island. Cuba freed itself of Spain but not the United States.

THE TEN YEARS' WAR AND ITS AFTERMATH

The timing of the rebellion coincided with the harsh rule of Captain-General Francisco Lersundi in Cuba and a period of political instability in Spain beginning with the deposal of Queen Isabella II in 1868. It was started by radical Creole landowners in Oriente Province under the leadership of Carlos Manuel de Céspedes from Bayamo. It was no accident that the rebellion began in the eastern part of the island as the plantations there were smaller and less modern than those of central Cuba. Plantation owners were generally poorer and lacked both modern machinery and the funds to purchase a large number of slaves. In fact, some had already experimented with freeing their slaves and paying them as contract labor during the *zafra* (sugar harvest). They had not benefited from the vast wealth generated from the Cuban bumper sugar crops in the 1860s. Rebellion was seen as a way to increase their wealth.

From his plantation on October 10, 1868, Céspedes issued his famous *Grito de Yara* proclaiming Cuban independence and freeing his slaves to serve in his rebel army. Céspedes cited several reasons for the rebellion against Spain. They included the inability of Cuban Creoles to serve in their own government, excessive taxation, corruption, the lack of religious liberties, suppression of the press and the denial of the rights of petition and assembly. Leaders in the eastern provinces in 1869 formed a provisional government with Céspedes as the president. Rebel leaders, such as Agnacio Agramonte from Camagüey, insisted on a legislative assembly with the ability to check the power of the president and to abolish slavery. Máximo Gómez, a Dominican, was selected as the leader of the rebel military forces because of his expertise in military strategy, in particular, guerrilla warfare. Gómez trained the mulatto leader Antonio Maceo, who became the most important rebel commander in the field.

Although many factors worked against the success of the Cuban rebels, the lack of unity and dissension within the rebel leadership were probably the most crucial. Leaders were divided over the issue of slavery. Céspedes urged slaves to revolt and join the rebels (*mambises*). This created a backlash by some wealthy, conservative Creole landowners who wanted independence but did not want to end slavery. Céspedes was later removed from office by the revolutionary legislative assembly and was killed by the Spanish in Oriente Province in 1874. The new rebel president, Salvador Cisneros Betancourt, a cattle rancher from Camagüey, and the next president, Tomás Estrada Palma, led rebel governments largely made up of conservative landowners. Many western landowners, especially sugar planters in Las Villas Province, remembering what had happened in Haiti, feared that Maceo would create a black republic after independence was won. They also feared that the scorched earth policies of Gómez and Maceo toward the sugar plantations in Oriente, if carried out in the central and western parts of the island, would destroy their wealth. This fear was heightened in early 1875 when Gómez burned eighty-three plantations around Sancti Spiritus and freed the slaves. In reaction to this, the rebel legislative assembly, now dominated by the more conservative Creole elites, was able to strip Gómez of many of his troops and prevent him from burning plantations in the prime sugar growing area of Cuba between Matanzas, Cárdenas and Colón. Some rebel leaders were jealous of Gómez's success and others resented the fact that a Dominican was in command of the rebel armies. Gómez was finally forced to resign his military post in 1876. He wrote in his diary, "I retired that same day with my heart broken by so many deceptions." Other factors also worked against the rebels. Weapons, supplies and money from exile groups in the United States arrived sporadically due to the fact that the U.S. government refused to recognize the movement for independence. It was difficult for the United States, which had just fought a civil war over the issue of slavery, to support a rebel movement in Cuba whose leadership was at best ambiguous and at worst divided on the issue of slavery. Finally, Spain controlled the sea-lanes and had a large number of troops in Cuba, thereby making it difficult for the rebels to win a major victory in the field. The rebels were largely limited to fighting a protracted, guerrilla war.

The bulk of the war was fought in the eastern part of the island. Maceo fought a successful guerrilla war against the larger Spanish forces. He gained the admiration of his own troops, fear from the Spanish troops and, at the same time, he became a threat to the more conservative rebel leadership who opposed him on the slavery issue. Maceo freed many slaves who rallied behind the rebel

cause in the east. The rebels controlled much of the eastern countryside while the Spanish controlled the cities. Neither side could
win a decisive victory. Brutality and arbitrary executions were
common. The symbol of the war became the machete. With the
political instability behind Spain in 1876, a new offensive led by
General Arsenio Martinez Campos was launched against the rebels. This offensive with more than 70,000 troops was coupled
with a diplomatic effort aimed at the more conservative elements
of the rebel leadership. Amnesty was guaranteed to all rebel
troops who surrendered before an end to the conflict. Rebel morale was very low by this time. An armistice, the Peace of Zanjon,
was finally agreed to in February 1878. Maceo refused to surrender. He wanted nothing less than Cuban independence and an
end to slavery. Facing the brunt of the Spanish forces alone with
his small army, Maceo realized he could not win. He traveled to
New York and worked with Calixto García in organizing a new
rebellion. This "little war" in 1879–1880 ended in disaster. After
ten long years of war, the Cuban people were not prepared to
fight anymore.

The war and the subsequent collapse in the world price of sugar
in the 1880s dramatically changed the political, economic and social systems of Cuba. Slavery was gradually phased out between
1879 and 1886. With slavery gone, the Creole landed elite no
longer had a reason to be loyal to Spain. Although voting was
limited due to property qualifications, Cubans were elected to the
Spanish Cortes and local councils. There was enormous property
damage to both the Creole loyalists and separatists. Very prominent separatist, Creole elite families had all their property seized
by the Spanish government. This included savings accounts,
stocks, bonds and personal property, as well as the cattle ranches,
tobacco farms, coffee estates and sugar plantations. The Spanish
government parceled out some of these seized plantations to par-
doned revolutionaries, soldiers who had served in the Spanish
army and Spanish immigrants.

The large sugar plantations that remained faced an uncertain
future. Almost all were severely in debt to bankers, shippers and
merchants. Interest rates skyrocketed. An 1880 law allowed creditors for the first time to seize the land of those planters who were
in default. According to historian Hugh Thomas, the U.S. consul
in Havana reported in 1884 that "out of the twelve or thirteen
hundred planters on the island, not a dozen are said to be sol-

vent." In that same year, sugar production had increased world-wide largely due to the development of the sugar beet industry in Europe. The price of sugar dropped dramatically. Many Cuban sugar plantations slipped into bankruptcy. It was clear that the smaller sugar plantations with the outdated sugar mills could no longer compete on the world market. It was also clear that significant changes were going to have to take place on the large sugar plantations. Cuba had no alternative but to turn to a more than willing United States for a market for its sugar and for capital. Capital was needed to modernize both the sugar industry and the economic infrastructure that supported it.

U.S. investors quickly took advantage of the situation in Cuba. U.S. companies acquired many Cuban and Spanish businesses, as well as many of the bankrupt tobacco and sugar plantations at rock-bottom prices. With this, the Cuban landed aristocracy—the Creole sugar elites—for the most part disappeared in the 1880s. U.S. capital and technology was used to modernize the sugar mills and make them more efficient. For example, Atkins and Company of Boston became the proprietors of the Soledad Plantation near Cienfuegos and several other surrounding plantations. By 1894, Atkins Soledad was one of the largest sugar plantations in the world with 12,000 total acres, 23 miles of private railroads, 5,000 acres of cane and 1,200 men employed at harvest time.[1] This *centrale* represented a combination of foreign capital, technology and efficiency that changed the social organization of sugar production in Cuba.

Most small sugar plantations could not afford to modernize their mills, so many simply began supplying cane to the *centrales.* Many of the large plantations with modern sugar mills leased their lands to tenants (*colonos*) who took care of growing the cane. In effect, there was now a division of labor between the cane growers (typically small farms and *colonos*) and the cane processors (*centrales*). Cheap U.S. steel allowed the *centrales* and the larger plantations to build private railways to get the cane to the mills more efficiently and to carry the processed sugar from the mills to the sea to private port facilities for export. By 1895, there were more than 350 miles of private railroads built in Cuba.[2] The *centrales* had access to capital and often made loans to the *colonos.* *Colonos* needed capital to pay wages, food and lodging for their workers and other costs. Small sugar planters and *colonos* were almost always in debt to the *centrale.* This created a patron-client relationship between the *centrales* and the *colonos*. *Centrales* began competing with each other for access to cane for the first time in Cuban history.

A growing sense of Cuban identity and nationalism was heightened by both the Ten Years' War and the realization by the Cubans after the war that Spain had no intention of allowing them to have any substantive say in its political and economic decisions. The rebel armies had been a mixture of rich and poor, black and white, peasant and workers, Chinese and mulatto. During the war, the words that would eventually become the Cuban national anthem were written and the Cuban flag first appeared. The machete became one of the nation's symbols. Although the bulk of the fighting was on the eastern part of the island, the fact that Creole leaders fought on parts of the island they had never seen before helped to overcome regional loyalties and develop a stronger sense of nationhood. By the early 1890s, the Autonomous Liberal Party of Cuba had become frustrated with Spain's lack of response to its demands for greater local control. Some Cuban nationalists, such as Martí, Gómez and Maceo, fled in exile to begin plotting their return and a new rebellion against Spain.

The McKinley Act of 1890 ended U.S. import duties on raw sugar and molasses. This greatly facilitated the growing trade between the United States and Cuba. By 1894, the United States had invested more than $50 million in Cuba, purchased 87 percent of Cuba's exports and accounted for almost 40 percent of the island's imports.[3] A downturn in the world's economy in the early 1890s reduced the demand for Cuban sugar. Many Cubans and American investors in Cuba came to blame Spanish imperial authority for their problems. The stage was set for another rebellion.

THE SECOND WAR OF INDEPENDENCE AND THE UNITED STATES

Martí, Gómez and Maceo arrived in Cuba in April 1895 to continue the rebellion against Spain. Estrada organized the Cuban exile community in the United States and began a public relations campaign to gain the support of the U.S. government. Although a revolutionary government was created, most decisions were made by the generals in the field. Martí was killed in a skirmish with Spanish forces near Bayamo in May. Making use of the expert horsemanship of their soldiers, living off the land and using guerrilla tactics they had developed during the Ten Years' War, Gómez and Maceo took the offensive. In September, Gómez and Maceo, leading rebel armies made up primarily of Africans and mulattos, expanded the war into the west. They reached Las Villas by November and were near Matanzas by Christmas. By January, Gómez was nearing Havana and Maceo was moving into the west into Pinar del Río Province. Gómez and Maceo once again employed scorched earth policies against the large plantations and *centrales*. When U.S. holdings were burned, many Americans complained to Estrada in the United States. He indicated that when the United States formally recognized the rebels, U.S. property would be protected. Recognizing the difficult situation, Spain sent General Valeriano Weyler to Havana to take control of its forces.

Estrada very effectively used the media to gain the support of the United States. With increasing competition for readership by the major newspapers (such as William Randolph Hearst's *New York Journal*) and the rise of yellow journalism in the United States, reports of Spanish cruelty and atrocities became commonplace as the American public began to demand that President Grover Cleveland do something about Cuba. General Fitzhugh Lee, the U.S. consul general in Havana and a nephew of Robert E. Lee, sympathized with the rebels and actively pushed for U.S. intervention into the war. By June, U.S. naval intelligence had prepared a war plan against Spain.

General Weyler concentrated on trying to isolate Maceo in the west. He hired Cuban counterguerrillas to fight against the rebels. He devised a plan in which people were forced into internment centers (concentration camps) throughout the island and anyone outside these centers was considered to be a rebel. Local Spanish commanders were given the power to execute rebels and anyone who refused to relocate to these centers. Rural villages and homes were destroyed by the Spanish. Planted fields were burned and livestock that could not be taken back to the internment centers was slaughtered. Anything that could possibly support the rebels was destroyed. Maceo and Gómez also waged a brutal war against the economic infrastructure and the large plantations that refused to contribute to their rebel forces. Maceo used his speed and maneuverability to avoid major battles with Weyler's larger forces. In April, Gómez ordered that all mill owners who continued to grind sugar cane should be hung. Some mill owners, including many U.S. owners, hired Spanish forces to protect them from the rebels.

By the middle of 1896, the Cuban economy had come to a standstill. Smallpox and yellow fever had reached epidemic proportions in areas where populations were interned, such as in Cienfuegos. Typhus, dysentery, cholera and measles raged through the 100,000 people who were interned in the shantytowns of Havana. By the end of 1896, the Spanish internment plan was beginning to work. Maceo was killed trying to break out into the central provinces as were several other rebel leaders throughout the island. Weyler controlled the western provinces of Pinar del Río, Havana and Matanzas by the end of February and by the middle of 1897 he had successfully cut the rebel leaders (Gómez, García and Quintin Banderas) off from each other. The rebels could no longer win the war, but they still had the capability of preventing a peaceful settlement and U.S. investments on the island continued to be vulnerable.

By now, General Weyler's reputation in the United States as a butcher appeared to make intervention likely. Recognizing the tremendous cost of trying to continue the war (Spain was also fighting a rebellion in the Philippines) and fearing U.S. intervention, the Spanish government changed its policy toward Cuba favoring limited autonomy within the Spanish empire, self-government and universal suffrage. General Weyler resigned and was replaced by Ramón Blanco. President William McKinley was open to the change in Spanish policy and a political settlement in Cuba. In fact, most U.S. businessmen who had investments in Cuba preferred a political settlement. Yet, the rebel leadership and most in Cuba could not accept a political settlement without complete independence—something that the Spanish government could not grant given its own unstable internal political situation. Rioting broke out in Havana by rebel supporters who were opposed to a limited political autonomy settlement. President McKinley believed that U.S. citizens and property were in danger. In January, he sent the battleship USS *Maine* to Havana and fate intervened.

On February 15, 1898, the *Maine* blew up in Havana harbor. Two hundred sixty men out of 355 died. Although the cause of the explosion was never satisfactorily explained, the sensationalistic U.S. press with its yellow journalism blamed Spain and created a near anti-Spanish hysteria within an American public that already disliked the Spanish. This hysteria played into the growing imperialistic desires of many leaders in the United States such as Theodore Roosevelt, the deputy secretary of the navy. President McKinley, desperately trying to avoid war, offered to buy Cuba from Spain for $300 million. Spain refused and McKinley capitulated to those who supported U.S. intervention. On April 19, the U.S. Congress demanded Spain give up its authority over Cuba. A U.S. blockade went into effect on April 21. Spain made overtures to the rebel commanders, but neither Gómez nor García were willing to accept. Gómez rejected an offer to join with Spain to "repel the North American invaders." He and García welcomed U.S. support, something Martí and Maceo probably would not have done if they had lived. The U.S. Congress declared war on Spain on April 25.

The fighting was over rather quickly. The U.S. Navy blockaded the outnumbered Spanish fleet in the harbor at Santiago. The demoralized Spanish troops fought bravely but were overwhelmed. In the most famous battle of the war at San Juan Hill in Santiago, the Spanish lost 102 men with 552 casualties. The United States lost almost 10 percent of its total forces—223 dead, 1,243 wounded and 79 missing—while Roosevelt and his Rough Riders became famous.[4] The Spanish fleet was sunk trying to run the blockade. Malaria, yellow fever and dysentery wreaked havoc with the U.S. troops. The Cuban forces under García were almost entirely African and mulatto while the American troops were almost all white. The Americans treated the Cubans with paternalistic contempt and, according to Hugh Thomas, in many ways preferred the company of the defeated Spanish to the black, "inferior and uncivilized" Cubans. U.S. General Rufus Shafter even suggested that they should serve as laborers rather than as soldiers in battle. Spanish General Juan José Toral surrendered in Santiago on July 17. The United States did not allow the black Cuban troops, who had fought the Spanish for three years, into the city to participate in the surrender ceremony. García himself refused an invitation to participate because the United States did not remove Spanish municipal authorities from power. The war ended officially on December 10 with the signing of the Treaty of Paris. Cuban officials were not asked to participate. The exclusion of Cubans from the decision-making process at the end of the war foreshadowed future Cuban relations with the United States.

Cuba had won its long struggle against Spain, but the cost was enormous. Almost two generations of Cuban families suffered directly from the thirty-year struggle. In the aftermath of the most recent struggle, thousands were left homeless and destitute. Those whose homes or farms had escaped the destruction of the war fell victim to tax collectors and creditors. Pawnshops proliferated. Entire families became beggars. The economy had come to a virtual halt. The economic infrastructure of the island had either been destroyed or was in disrepair. Almost one-third of the sugar plantations had been burned through the scorched earth policies of the armies. Matanzas Province, the center of sugar production, had virtually collapsed with the number of operating mills falling from 400 in 1894 to 62 in 1898. Only 207 sugar mills on the entire island were operating at the end of the war. This was down from 1,100 working mills in 1894.[5] The few remaining sugar elites were heavily in debt and could not make their mortgage payments. Literally thousands of small farms, cattle ranches, tobacco farms and coffee farms disappeared. General Lee said, "The great fertile island of Cuba in some places resembled an ash pile, in others the dreary desert." It was estimated that more than two-thirds of Cuban wealth had been consumed during the war. Given its vulnerable situation and desperate needs, Cuba was unable to counter the growing power and manifest destiny of the United States.

OCCUPATION AND CONDITIONAL INDEPENDENCE

Cuba was placed under U.S. military occupation led by General John Brooke from January until December 1899 and then under General Leonard Wood until May 1902. The United States did not allow the Cuban rebel army to participate in the final Spanish exit from the island in ceremonies held in Havana and Santiago. The stated reason for this insult was the possible threat to life and property should the victory celebrations become excessive and end up as riots, although it was clear that the U.S. belief in its mission of bringing civilization to the "inferior" people of Latin America played a role in the nature of its policies toward the Cuban people. The policies often reflected arrogance, paternalism and racism that upset many Cuban nationalists. But, given the harsh economic and political realities of 1899, there was nothing they could do.

The U.S. occupation had three interrelated goals: to maintain political stability, to rebuild the primary economic infrastructure of the island to attract U.S. investments and to keep Cuba within the sphere of influence of the growing political and economic power of the United States. The U.S. military appropriated the Cuban treasury and its public revenues. The exhausted rebel army, which had not been paid, disbanded when the United States offered to purchase its equipment and weapons. It also helped that certain rebel leaders were offered well-paid positions within the new administrative structure. The United States created a Rural Guard, the majority of which were non-Africans who had served in the rebel armies. It was designed primarily to protect U.S. property in rural areas. The judicial branch of the Cuban government was reorganized and an electoral system was established that gave the vote to male property owners. Three parties, the Republicans, the Nationalists and the Union Democratica competed for municipal elections in June. The Republicans, led by former rebel commander José Gómez and based in Santa Clara, favored immediate independence. The Nationalists, led by former rebel General Máximo Gómez and based in Havana, favored immediate independence and a strong central government. The Union Democratica consisted of former Autonomistas and expected annexation to the United States.

Roads, bridges and railways were rebuilt. Port facilities were improved. Food distribution was an immediate priority and the United States focused on improving the health and education sectors of Cuba. Hospitals were built and the sanitary and health conditions improved in many areas of the island. The American Sanitary Commission eradicated yellow fever, although its success was based largely on the research of Cuban scientist Carlos Finlay, who correctly linked the disease to mosquitoes. General Wood, who believed the Cubans would ask to be annexed to the United States, began to reorganize the education system based on the U.S. public school model. Cuban teachers adopted U.S. teaching methods and U.S. textbooks were translated into Spanish and adopted by the schools, although no attempt was made to make them understandable within the Cuban culture and context.

Cuban business owners and farmers appealed to the U.S. military for assistance such as low-interest loans or subsidies to make it through the difficult economic times. All were rejected by General Brooke, who argued that these types of public subsidies and charities would do nothing but encourage dependence, increase pauperism and destroy an individual's self-respect. Cuban property owners were forced into bankruptcy. Between 1898 and 1900, farms changed owners at a rate of almost 4,000 a year.[6] Estates were abandoned and property values fell dramatically. Land could be purchased at one-tenth to one-twentieth of its value prior to the rebellion. Thousands of Americans came to Cuba looking to purchase land cheaply and make their fortunes.

In September 1900, thirty-one delegates were elected to participate in a constitutional convention for Cuba. The Cuban constitution that was developed called for universal suffrage for all males, a complete separation of church and state, a powerful presidency and a weak legislative branch. General Wood, who doubted the ability of Cubans to govern and had already antagonized former rebel leaders, wanted a provision in the new constitution or a treaty that would spell out the future relationship between the United States and Cuba. General Wood made this recommendation to Elihu Root, the U.S. secretary of war. Root wanted to secure U.S. rights of intervention to maintain an "adequate government" in Cuba. An adequate government meant one that was stable, fiscally responsible, would not enter into agreements with European powers that might "interfere with the independence of Cuba," would allow the United States the right to intervene to protect Cuban independence and would allow the United States to maintain a naval presence on the island. He then recommended to Secretary of State John Hay that the new Cuban constitution should spell out this relationship between Cuba and the United States. This came to be known as the Platt Amendment to the Cuban constitution. It allowed the United States to intervene into the domestic politics of Cuba whenever it believed the government lacked the ability to govern or should its independence ever be threatened. In 1901, the Cuban constitutional convention voted sixteen to eleven with four abstentions to accept the Platt Amendment without any modifications, largely due to President McKinley's threat of not withdrawing the U.S. Army from Cuba and Root's effective diplomacy and characterization of the amendment as simply a restatement of the Monroe Doctrine.

General Wood used money from the Cuban treasury to mount a public relations campaign in the United States to encourage investment in both the sugar and tobacco industries and to lower U.S. tariffs on these products. Before 1899, almost all tobacco companies were either Cuban or Spanish owned. By May 1902, North American companies controlled more than 90 percent of the export trade in Cuban cigars and more than 50 percent of the manufacture of Cuban cigars and cigarettes. The United Fruit Company of Boston created the first great sugar *centrale* (called Boston) in Cuba on the edge of the Bay of Banes. In 1900, it invested more than $20 million in Cuba. Texas investor R. B. Hawley and former Cuban general Mario García Menocal created the Cuban American Company and built the *centrale* Chaparra on the north coast of Oriente. It became the largest sugar estate in the world.[7] General Wood then maneuvered to gain the support of the U.S. Congress to lower the tariff on Cuban sugar. Wood also granted more than 218 mining concessions to U.S. companies, who were exempted from property taxes. By 1902, U.S. investment capital in Cuba totaled more than $100 million and by 1905 nearly 13,000 Americans had bought land in Cuba.[8]

In December 1901, Estrada was elected the first president of the Republic of Cuba and on May 20, 1902, the Cuban flag was raised for the first time over Cuba. By this time, the United States had already replaced Spain as a point of reference for most Cubans. Cuba was now independent, but the stage was set for the United States to dominate the political and economic processes of the island and to reshape its politics, economics, society, culture and identity. Martí's dream of a truly independent Cuba remained just that—a dream.

JOSÉ MARTÍ

José Martí—a literary figure, poet, revolutionary and freedom fighter—is considered to be the father figure of modern Cuba. He was born in 1853. His father, who was a city official and a policeman in Havana, was from Valencia and his mother from the Canary Islands. He was influenced throughout school by Rafael Maria Mendive, an educator, poet and prominent supporter of Cuban independence. Martí founded his first newspaper, *Patria Libre,* in 1869 and was exiled to Spain due to his proindependence activities. While in Spain, he studied law and wrote articles and poems about national independence. He traveled to Mexico where he established himself as a literary figure and a supporter of an independent Cuba. He returned to Cuba in 1878–1879 before ending up in New York with the exiled Cuban community. For the next ten years, he was a creator and leader of the Cuban Revolutionary Committee of New York and wrote many articles and poems concerning Cuban independence. It was Martí who laid the groundwork for Cuban independence through his intense opposition to the idea of the U.S. annexation of Cuba and his distrust of the Autonomistas. He became so well known throughout Latin America that he was not only a vice consul for Uruguay, but also for Argentina and Paraguay. Martí organized Cuban American tobacco workers in Florida to contribute monetarily to the cause of Cuba Libre. By this time, it was clear that Martí was not only concerned about independence from Cuba, but also from the United States. He was witness to the growing economic and military power of the United States, coupled with an expansionistic, missionary belief system that found an outlet in the newspaper industry led by Hearst. Martí then enlisted the military support of Gómez and Maceo and returned to Cuba in 1895 to renew the Cuban struggle for independence. Martí died in a small battle near Bayamo in May and became a martyr to Cuba Libre. He was the foremost spokesperson for Cuban independence. He feared that Cuba would win its independence from Spain only to lose it to the United States. He wrote, "It is my duty . . . to prevent through the independence of Cuba, the U.S.A. from spreading over the West Indies." The Platt Amendment was a confirmation of Martí's worst fear. The Cuban wars of independence were lost to the United States.

NOTES

1. Hugh Thomas, *Cuba; the Pursuit of Freedom* (New York: Harper and Row, 1971), 274.
2. Ibid., 274.
3. Ibid., 289.
4. Ibid., 393.
5. Ibid., 425.
6. Louis A. Pérez Jr., *On Becoming Cuban* (Chapel Hill: University of North Carolina Press, 1999), 106.
7. Thomas, *Cuba; the Pursuit of Freedom*, 466–468.
8. Ibid., 466, 600.

4

U.S. Dominance, the Failure of Reform and the Rise of Batista: 1902 to 1952

Politics and economics are so intertwined that it is impossible to understand one without the other. Nowhere is this more evident than in the history of Cuba during the first half of the twentieth century. The Platt Amendment and the growing political and economic power of the United States made a mockery of Cuban independence. Cuba was strategically important because it allowed the United States to control access to the Panama Canal. The United States also believed that the maintenance of political stability, although not necessarily democracy, was the best way to protect its growing economic investments and its dominance of the Cuban sugar industry. U.S. trade agreements with Cuba encouraged the export of sugar and, in effect, restricted the diversification of the Cuban economy.

Given its increasing dependence on the export of sugar, the Cuban economy was acutely vulnerable to changes in the world market price. Economic hard times were often associated with political instability on the island. Labor unrest was common. Political instability was viewed as a direct threat to the Cuban political and economic elites and, perhaps more importantly, to U.S. investments on the island. Cuban elites came to rely on a politicized army and a more than willing United States to maintain political stability. Corruption became pervasive and the standard way of doing business in Cuba. Politics became a way of accumulating wealth and, thus, elections often turned into political crises that invited U.S. intervention.

When the corrupt and repressive Gerardo Machado became a second-term president through fraudulent elections in 1928, students entered the Cuban political scene as the heirs to José Martí's dream of a truly independent Cuba. Student-led reform peaked with Ramón Grau San Martín becoming president in 1933. Grau's nationalistic reforms, pro-labor policies and proposals for agrarian reform were opposed by forces on the right such as the United States, the Cuban military and economic elites and those on the left that included radical students who claimed his reforms were much too moderate. Political instability at this time marked the entry of the military as the decisive actor in the political decision-making processes of Cuba. By 1934, the United States came to see Fulgencio Batista and the military as the only guarantee for the necessary political stability and the protection of the vast U.S. interests on the island.

Growing wealth during World War II created a surplus of government revenue that allowed political elites to pay for modest social reforms while elite patronage, corruption and graft worsened. Economic growth created a growing middle class that adopted an American consumer culture with rising economic expectations and the hope of political reform. Batista would end the hope of meaningful political reform with the *golpe* (illegal takeover of the government either by the military or with the support of the military) of 1952 and the rising economic expectations would never be fulfilled due to the inability of the sugar industry to provide the necessary economic growth on the island by the middle of the 1950s.

CUBA DURING THE PLATT AMENDMENT YEARS

Tomás Estrada Palma, a former teacher, rebel president and leader of the Cuban exiles in the United States, was elected without opposition as the first president of the newly independent

Cuba. He curried favor with the United States and used patronage to maintain the support of various elite groups. Corruption, intimidation, fraud and graft became a staple of his administration. In 1903, the Commercial Treaty of Reciprocity gave Cuban sugar and other agricultural products exported to the United States a 20 percent tariff preference and gave American products preferential treatment when exported to Cuba. This facilitated a growing American presence on the island that could be seen in clothing fashions, education, architecture, business practices, sport and leisure and the growth of language schools specializing in English. In the same year, Cuba agreed to lease Bahia Honda and Guantánamo Bay to the United States. Guantánamo Bay would serve as a coaling station and naval base for the United States.

The 1904 elections for the Cuban national legislature were marred by fraud and in 1905 Estrada intimidated his opponent into withdrawing from the election and was reelected president. The Liberal Party led by José Miguel Gómez and veterans of Cuba Libre cried foul and organized a rebellion. The rebels had 15,000 troops in the field against Havana by the end of August and destroyed the communications network of the island so as to isolate the small Rural Guard units. The Rural Guard, created by the United States during its first occupation of the island, amounted to nothing more than police units designed to protect the property of wealthy landowners and was not capable of fighting the rebels. Not having a standing army to counter the rebels, Estrada asked President Theodore Roosevelt for support. Roosevelt dispatched Secretary of War William Taft to Havana to negotiate a settlement between the two parties. Taft was unimpressed with Estrada and believed that he should resign. He also came to the conclusion that none of the Liberals were capable of governing the country. Estrada and his supporters in the Cuban legislature resigned on September 28, 1906, and effectively left Cuba without a government. Two thousand U.S. Marines landed in Havana the next day. Taft commented that the Cuban government had "proven to be nothing but a house of cards." Cuba was once again occupied by the United States.

Roosevelt placed Charles Magoon, the former governor of the Panama Canal Zone, in charge of the American occupation. Magoon, with support from the Liberals, created a permanent standing army while preserving the function of the Rural Guard. Magoon believed that a large standing army would serve to deter any internal rebellion and provide the necessary political stability for U.S. strategic and economic interests while the Rural Guard would continue to function primarily as a police force to protect private property. It was believed that this standing army would eliminate the need for the use of U.S. troops in Cuba. The United States provided supplies, weapons, training and advisers to the Cuban military. Cuban officers began attending service academies in the United States. Magoon also reformed the electoral system by developing qualifications for voters and candidates for public office. Election boards were created to maintain the lists of eligible voters. A racist immigration policy was adopted by favoring "whites," in particular Spaniards, and restricting "races of color" into Cuba. The sinecure system was expanded to pacify elite groups within Cuba and by the time the Americans left in 1909, elite opposition to U.S. dominance had, for the most part, come to an end. Magoon granted several major public works contracts to American firms and continued to work on infrastructure improvements such as roads to the tobacco-growing region of Pinar del Río. Local elections were held in August 1908 and national elections in November. Not surprisingly, Gómez, the Liberal Party candidate, was elected president and the U.S. occupation ended with Magoon leaving on the newly rebuilt battleship USS *Maine*.

With a cock on a plough as the symbol of the Liberal Party, Miguel Gómez, in one of his first public acts, reinstated the traditional rural social pastime of cockfighting. Public corruption and graft increased, especially in the awarding of government contracts for infrastructure improvements such as sewage and water systems, railroads, roads, telephone lines, bridges, port facilities and military barracks. Underpaid public officials viewed graft (*chivo*) as a way of supplementing their incomes. Cuban newspapers received government subsidies or grants and could not be relied on for objective reporting. The national lottery was reinstated and provided the government with money for patronage purposes. Officers in the army who were loyal to Estrada were dismissed. Officer appointments and commissions were based on loyalty to the ruling Liberal Party, although factions appeared between the supporters of Gómez (Miguelistas) and the supporters of Vice President Alfredo Zayas (Zayistas). This practice of politicizing the military came to be a permanent feature in Cuban politics and served to undermine its professionalism, discipline and morale.

The U.S. government periodically reminded Gómez that failure to protect life and property of U.S. investors could lead to an intervention. The army was used to meet the needs of the rural landowners. Calvary units patrolled the sugar districts during the *zafra*. The United States continued to influence and in some cases to interfere in the decision-making process on the island. For example, President Taft squelched an attempt by Great Britain to gain a contract to build a railroad between Nuevitas and Caibarien. He offered new loans to the Cuban government with conditions that increased U.S. control over the Cuban treasury and he finalized the Guantánamo Treaty in December 1912, which gave the United States a naval base on the island for a total rent of $2,000 a year.

The Independent Party of Color (Partido Independiente de Color; PIC) had been organized in 1908 in response to growing complaints against the dominance of the economy by foreigners (not only Spaniards who were favored in the immigration policies, but also Americans who dominated the sugar industry) and white Cuban elites. The primary purpose of the party was to defend the interests of black Cubans. Black or mulatto Cubans made up about 30 percent of the population in 1907 and were the majority in the relatively large cities of Santiago, Jovellanos and Guantánamo. Blacks and mulattos had twice the illiteracy rate as whites, were underrepresented in the professions and most practiced either African religions or religions that represented a syncretism between Catholicism and the African religions.[1] PIC was led by Evaristo Estenoz, a former slave and veteran of Cuba Libre and the Liberal Party uprising of 1906. With the passage of a law in the Cuban senate that banned all political parties based on race, PIC led an uprising consisting largely of labor strikes and demonstrations throughout the island on May 20, 1912. Panic spread, especially in Havana, where the fear of the "Negro uprising" was greatest. The army was able to put down the uprising rather quickly except in Oriente Province where the largest number of blacks and mulattos lived. The United States, fearing destruction of American property, sent the battleship USS *Nebraska* to Havana and landed U.S. Marines in Daiquiri (Oriente Province) on May 31. Four thousand blacks under the command of Estenoz were defeated in a battle in June and the uprising quickly disintegrated. This was the last race-based uprising in Cuba. After this defeat, black or Afro-Cuban elites and politicians tended to associate with the existing political structure. The vast majority were never integrated into the general political development of the island.

The Liberal Party split between supporters of Gómez and Zayas led to the election of Cornell University–educated General Mario García Menocal as president in 1913. He was the manager of the huge Chaparra sugar mill and plantation and leader of the Conservative Party. Menocal, who had strong support by the U.S. government, was even more corrupt than Gómez. He pursued several loans from the United States and began a purge of Liberal Party supporters within the military. With the beginning of the world war in 1914, European sugar beet production came to a standstill and the world market price of sugar almost doubled during the months of July and August. That year, three *centrales* were founded and the next year twelve new mills were built with U.S. companies owning eight of them. A total of twenty-one new mills were built between 1907 and 1919, most taking advantage of new U.S. technology using multiple rollers and electricity. This allowed Cuba to become the largest exporter of sugar in the world.

More land came under sugar production, including some of the virgin forests of cedar, mahogany and mastic in Pinar del Río. This led to a labor shortage and the need to import laborers from Haiti, Jamaica and China. Another outcome of the Cuban sugar boom was the merger of sugar mills and plantations with companies that were large users of sugar such as Coca-Cola, Hershey and Hires (root beer).[2] Hershey even purchased the Havana-Matanzas electric railway. American ownership of sugar mills increased to an estimated 35 to 50 percent of all the sugar mills in Cuba. The Cuban Cane Sugar Corporation founded in New York purchased fourteen mills in 1916 that included the following *centrales:* Conchita, Asunción, Mercedes, San Ignacio, Agramonte, Jaguayal and Lugareno. By 1918, it was the largest sugar enterprise in the world.[3] The sugar boom brought prosperity to the island. Conspicuous consumption could be seen in the wealthy Havana districts of Vedado and Miramar. Cars could be seen regularly on the streets of Havana and the tourist industry developed around gambling.

Continued divisions within the Liberal Party coupled with a fraudulent election count allowed Menocal, the U.S. favorite, to win reelection in 1916. Violence marked the election. Candidates and election board officials were shot. As many as fifty people died in preelection violence. In the end, Menocal won an election in which more votes were cast than the number of people who were eligible to vote. Miquelista and Zayista military officers with Liberal Party politicians plotted a *golpe* against Menocal and the Conservatives in 1917. Even though they were able to seize control of Camagüey and Santiago for a short period, the *golpe* failed largely due to their inability to seize the main military camps (Camp Columbia and La Cabana) in Havana. Five hundred U.S. Marines landed in Santiago and occupied Guantánamo, El Cobre, Manzanillo and Nuevitas. This failed *golpe* allowed Menocal to continue to fill the military with his loyalists. With U.S. encouragement, Menocal declared that Cuba would no longer be neutral in the ongoing conflict in Europe. He used the excuse of world war as a reason to continue to exercise the near dictatorial powers he had adopted during the *golpe* attempt. Menocal's corruption knew no boundaries as imaginary roads and bridges were built over rivers that did not exist. Government officials ran their own businesses with money from the treasury. U.S. Marines remained in the country until 1923.

In the 1920 election, Zayas, who had been expelled from the Liberal Party by Gómez, was elected by joining forces with the Conservative Party under Menocal. Menocal's support was won with the promise that Zayas would support him in the 1924 election. Menocal was also able to buy off Gervasio Sierra, the leader of the growing trade unionists. The threat of officer purges should the Liberals win the election was used to gain military support for Zayas. The military harassed and intimidated Liberal Party leaders and voters. In some areas, the military was used to supervise and rig the election outcome. This effectively eliminated the power of the Liberal governors in these areas. In some areas, more votes were cast than there were voters. By this time, it was clear to all that the Cuban military could determine the outcome of an election.

During World War I, an international committee made up of representatives from the United States and Great Britain supervised the sugar supply to the allies. By 1918, it had basically set the world market price of sugar at 4.6 cents a pound and purchased the entire Cuban crop.[4] This was much higher than the prewar price but lower than what could have been obtained in a free market situation. Price controls ended in 1920 and the "Dance of the Millions" began. The price of sugar escalated from 9 cents a pound in February to 22 cents a pound in May. The price of sugar then collapsed as quickly as it had risen. By December, it had fallen to less than 4 cents a pound. This devastated most of the sugar mills that had contracted to purchase large quantities of sugar at high prices and borrowed money to expand operations based on the promise of higher prices. Then, when the price of sugar dramatically fell, they were faced with having to sell their processed sugar at a much lower price. Many went bankrupt and could not pay off their loans. By the end of 1921, the First National City Bank of New York had foreclosed on more than sixty sugar mills in Cuba.

The economic crisis caused many big investors to withdraw their accounts from Cuban banks who were already overextended in loans. The entire banking system was near collapse when the U.S. government sent Albert Rathbone, a financial adviser, to Cuba in December 1920. Rathbone stayed two weeks, recommended a U.S. loan to the Cuban banking system and billed the Cuban government $50,000 for his services. The United States sent Special Ambassador Enoch Crowder to Havana in January on the battleship USS *Minnesota*. The National Bank of Cuba closed its doors in April 1921 with its debts exceeding its ability to pay by more than $65 million. One month after the inauguration of Zayas in May, eighteen Cuban banks had collapsed with a combined debt of $130 million. Government workers and teachers went unpaid.[5]

The United States made a difficult situation worse when it raised its tariff on Cuban sugar by a little more than one cent a pound. This was largely due to the growing influence of the American sugar beet industry. By September, tons of unsold sugar remained in Cuba. The situation was critical. Zayas agreed to cut the Cuban budget and a group of U.S. banks under the direction of J. P. Morgan provided a short-term emergency loan of $5 million until a long-term financial package could be worked out. Cuba's sugar crop of 1921 sold for less than it had generated in 1915 even though it was the second largest crop in the history of the country. A financial package from the United States was contingent on Zayas meeting some of the reforms demanded by Crowder. Crowder insisted on reform of the lottery, the firing of the "corrupt" members of Zayas's cabinet and further budget cuts. New York bankers under Morgan also insisted that Crowder must stay on in Cuba for another two years as ambassador. Zayas agreed and was awarded a major financial aid package consisting of a $50 million loan to keep the government running and pay its employees, a $7 million loan to pay Cuba's war debts and $6 million for public works debts. With this financial package, the corrupt Zayas enriched himself, his family and supporters and maneuvered to put his own people back in his cabinet.

The economic problems of Cuba resulted in a growing nationalism that expressed itself in resentment toward U.S. interference into Cuban affairs, demands to repeal the Platt Amendment, opposition to the growing U.S. economic presence and support for tariffs to protect and promote Cuban businesses. Newspaper articles and cartoons depicted Zayas as a puppet of the United States. This nationalism would eventually spill over into the demands for an end to the massive political corruption and a call for greater social justice on the island. Zayas was able to take advantage of this nationalism and negotiate the return of the Isle of Pines to Cuban control. U.S.-controlled sugar companies in Cuba urged the United States to stop an attempt by the Cuban senate to close all private railways and ports. A compromise brought about an end to the construction of all private railroads and ports after 1923.

Various groups began calling for more progressive policies, such as increased taxation on the wealthy, a national healthcare system, government control of the sugar industry, a new trade treaty with the United States and an end to the massive political corruption. The Havana Federation of Workers organized strikes in favor of better wages and working conditions. Faculty at the University of Havana complained of Cuba's educational backwardness and began demanding greater support for university programs that would be more attuned to the development needs of the island. University students were not only influenced by their faculty, but also by the Mexican and Russian revolutions and the success of the students in Argentina during the Cordoba reform movement. They began to speak out for the less privileged sectors of Cuban society. A University Student Federation (Federacíon Estudiantil Universitaria; FEU) was organized in 1923 and student leader Julio Antonio Mella became a national figure. A nationalistic literature, journalism and music scene developed that was led by scholars and writers such as Fernando Ortiz, Carlos Trelles, Ruben Martinez Villena and Jorge Manach and composers such as Amado Roldan.

The corrupt Zayas benefited from a 4-million-ton sugar harvest in 1922 and an increase in the world market price of sugar in 1923 to 5 cents a pound. Sugar would not command this price again until 1956. Cuban sugar production topped 4 million tons in 1924 at a price of 3.82 cents a pound and 5 million tons in 1925 at a price less than 3 cents a pound. In the 1924 election, the Conservatives nominated Menocal again while Zayas threw his support to the Liberal Party candidate Gerardo Machado. Machado, a former cattle thief, member of Gómez's cabinet, vice president of the American-owned Cuban Electric Company and owner of the Moulin Rouge Theatre, won the fraudulent election by promising "roads, water and schools" for Cuba.

By this time, American influences in Cuba were readily visible. U.S. racist policies that were put in place during the first occupation (1898–1902) continued to have an impact on the social norms of the island. Resident Americans and businesses openly practiced discrimination against mulattoes and Afro-Cubans. This practice was increasingly found among Cuban businesses as well. The Cuban government openly discriminated against Cubans of color in its hiring practices. American tourism increased dramatically from 33,000 in 1914 to 56,000 in 1920 to 90,000 in 1928.[6] New U.S.-owned hotels and restaurants catered to American tourist interests. Cuban-owned hotels were often managed by Americans. During the American prohibition era, large numbers of bartenders and bar owners moved to Havana. U.S. tourist agencies advertised Cuba as a tropical paradise where Americans could indulge themselves in actions that were forbidden at home—gambling, playing the lottery, drinking or romancing with an exotic lover. Horse racing, boxing, prostitution and baseball became prominent features of the Cuban landscape. American films were well known and became extremely popular throughout Cuba. A U.S. company created the first theater chain on the island and by 1920 Havana had more than forty movie theaters. Movie advertisements helped sell American beauty products, clothes, cigarettes, breakfast foods, beverages and detergents. U.S. department store chains, such as Woolworth's, appeared in major Cuban cities. The rapid expansion of electrical power during the 1920s fed the growing demand for American appliances such as toasters, electric clocks, mixers and fans. Radios became a highly sought after item for almost all Cubans. In a case study of General Electric in Cuba, historian Thomas F. O'Brien traces the transfer of American corporate culture and values in Cuba such as modern management and production techniques. At the same time, he provides evidence of the standard American racist view of the natural inferiority of Cuban workers.[7]

U.S. companies outside of Havana made their presence felt as well. They came to own vast tracts of land. Comfortable, modern and well-kept American communities sprang up near the U.S. companies all across the island. These communities isolated themselves from Cuban life, preferring to maintain the American way of life rather than becoming part of Cuba. Cuban employees sometimes lived in company towns in which the company owned and provided virtually everything including housing, retail and food stores and loan facilities. The best (or worst) examples of this existed at the large American sugar mills with their segregated American and Cuban zones. The sugar mill was the dominant force in these areas providing virtually all the local employment and becoming a transmitter of American values. In addition to working as laborers and as low- to midlevel administrators, Cubans were hired as surveyors, accountants, clerks, teachers, engineers, technicians and physicians for the mill. The local holidays and social calendar set by the sugar mill typically reflected American holidays and events. Stores managed by the sugar mill sold almost exclusively American products. Cubans came to adopt the American consumer culture. The sugar mill and its surrounding area was a self-contained region capable of providing its own law enforcement. The mill provided grants and contributions to local towns to build schools, libraries and roads. It provided scholarships to send the children of its employees to universities. Yet, this came at a price. Local Cubans became totally dependent on the sugar mill. With dependency also came a sense of powerlessness. Workers had no recourse to arbitrary dismissals. Mill owners fought labor organizers. Locals working in the mill administration rarely moved beyond midlevel positions that were reserved for Americans. They endured the humiliation of racist remarks by the American employees. Finally, the mill was in a position to make deals with the corrupt, local political elites. The mill could do as it pleased in Cuba. As historian Louis A. Pérez Jr. points out, "The sugar company was emblematic of almost everything that was wrong in Cuba's relationship with the United States: the powerlessness, the degree to which the mill constituted a world into itself in which Cubans had no rights except those conceded by the company and to which existed neither remedy nor redress."

MACHADO AND THE GENERATION OF 1930

Machado quickly moved to gain both control and support of the military and the opposition politicians. Military officers supportive of Menocal were quickly retired and replaced with *machadistas*. Promotions and appointments were contingent on loyalty to the governing party. Other officers were bribed with extra pay and benefits. The few professional Cuban officers educated at U.S. military schools found their authority undermined by Machado, who frequently turned to the "interests" of the noncommissioned officers—the sergeants—for his support. Machado increased the military budget and the number of soldiers, built new training facilities, created an air corps and improved the housing conditions on military bases. The military began supervising physical education and marching classes in the secondary schools. Graft within the military increased as it controlled the production, distribution and sale of meat and milk throughout Cuba. Kickbacks from private companies who supplied the military became common. With the promise of an arrangement (*cooperativismo*) for sharing the graft and control of the lottery, most of the old politicians from the "independence generation" in the legislature, including many of the Conservatives, were bought off by Machado. In this way, he came to control the competition among Cuban elites. Those that did not support this arrangement were sent into exile. Machado banned opposition parties. He began an extensive public works program with work on the Central Highway in 1927 while a private building boom in Havana had also started. His decision to seek an extra term was met with student demonstrations and riots and labor unrest across the island. Machado quickly closed the university and exiled the Spanish labor leaders as undesirable aliens. Endorsed by President Calvin Coolidge, Machado won an uncontested, fraudulent election in 1928.

The Great Depression devastated the export-oriented sugar-dominated Cuban economy. By 1929, the price of sugar was down to 1.79 cents per pound and by 1932 to .72 cents a pound. The Smoot-Hawley Tariff, which added 2 cents per pound on sugar exported to the United States in 1930, effectively cut Cuba's share of the U.S. sugar market in half by 1933.[8] Economic hard times set the environment for the growing opposition to the increasingly repressive Machado government and his secret police, the *porra*. This also alarmed the United States. The opposition to Machado centered along two major groups that were outside his governing arrangement of *cooperativismo*—labor and students. This opposition took the form of an urban underground that waged a war consisting of strikes, work stoppages, demonstrations, assassinations, gun battles, bombings, riots and propaganda.

Students, many of whom were the sons, grandsons, daughters or granddaughters of those that had fought in Cuba Libre, had entered the political arena during the Zayas administration with the formation of the FEU. In 1927, the University Student Directorate (Directorio Estudiantil Universitario; DEU) was formed in reaction to Machado's decision to seek another term. It organized a large demonstration in September 1930 that ended in a riot and the death of DEU leader Rafael Trejo. Machado closed the university and all high schools across the island. According to Cuban historian Jaime Suchlicki, it was the martyrdom of Trejo that led most Cubans to come to support the student opposition to Machado. This student opposition movement came to be known as the Generation of 1930. A more radical and secretive group led by middle-class professionals called the ABC (note that the meaning of the letters is unknown; the group was simply known as the ABC) was founded in 1931 with the goal of killing Machado. This group, led by Harvard-educated Cuban intellectuals, adopted the terrorist technique of assassination through bombings and published a manifesto demanding limits on U.S. control of Cuban land, nationalization of public services and an end to large landholdings on the island.

Labor or working-class groups in Cuba were located primarily in the export-oriented foreign-owned industries, so that labor unrest was not simply a domestic issue. Labor unrest among the tobacco, sugar, construction, railroad and dock workers brought the possibility of U.S. intervention and had historically been repressed by the various Cuban governments after independence. Prior to 1925, Cuban labor was typically tied to or led by veterans of the Spanish anarcho-syndicalist labor movement. It is also important to note that rural (primarily workers on the sugar plantations) and urban workers often maintained contact each other. This made it possible for a unified labor movement that could be mobilized for political purposes if a Cuban leader could somehow capture control of it. The Confederacion Nacional Obrera Cubana (CNOC), the first national labor organization, was created in 1925 and had 71,000 members by 1929. The CNOC included the newly created communist party of Cuba known as the Union Revolucionaria Comunista (URC) which in 1944 was renamed the Popular Socialist Party (Partido Socialista Popular; PSP). It was led by the Spanish communist Jose Miguel Pérez and student leader Antonio Mella. Machado responded with violence to strikes by textile and railway workers in 1925. The secretary general of the CNOC was literally thrown to the sharks by Machado's secret police the following year. Machado continued to assassinate militant labor leaders while trying, unsuccessfully, to capture control of the labor organizations. As the depression deepened, labor became more militant and 200,000 workers went on strike in March 1930. Although numbering only 100 members in 1929, the URC gained control of the majority of the leadership positions within the CNOC by 1931.

The Cuban military was called on by Machado to carry out more and more of the repression against the opposition. Those charged with activities against the government were often tried in military courts. Students and faculty members of the University of Havana were arrested on charges of conspiracy to overthrow the government in early 1931. Among them was Ramón Grau San Martín, a popular physiology professor. The ABC, the DEU, the URC and the CNOC responded to Machado's increasing violence with more violence of their own. Daily political murders and increasing urban violence coupled with a disastrous sugar harvest characterized the Cuba of 1932. Unemployment was at an all-time high. The United States gave Machado emergency loans to pay Cuba's debts. In September, the ABC assassinated the president of the Cuban senate. This was followed by an unprecedented campaign of terror against students and the other opposition groups. In January 1933, more than 20,000 sugar workers went on strike and it was evident that by that time the army was the only institution that kept Machado in power. It was against this backdrop that the United States and newly elected President Franklin Roosevelt decided it was necessary to act. Fearing a threat to American investments and being lobbied by exiled Cuban elites, Roosevelt sent Sumner Welles to mediate between Machado and the opposition in May. Welles's decision to talk to the opposition legitimized these groups and empowered them to play a major role in a post-Machado government. When Machado rejected the mediation efforts, Welles threatened to withdraw U.S. support for the government and hinted at the possibility of an armed U.S. intervention.

A bus driver's strike in Havana during the summer culminated in a general strike across the island in early August. According to Suchlicki, the URC lost all credibility, especially with students, during the general strike because it made a last-minute deal with Machado promising to call off the strike. The URC believed it could head off an immediate U.S. intervention on the island that would result in a pro-U.S. government. In the passion of the moment, the workers ignored the return-to-work order. For the next twenty-five years, the discredited communists worked primarily with the more conservative forces and the military in Cuba.

By the end of the first week of August, Cuba was ready to collapse into anarchy. Welles suggested a plan in which Machado and all his cabinet would resign except General Alberto Herrera, the secretary of war, who would become the interim president until a civilian could be selected. Realizing that the United States no longer backed Machado, the Cuban military became concerned about its repressive activities in support of Machado and there was a growing fear of an antimilitary backlash in a newly constituted Cuban government. After receiving a promise from Welles and the other opposition leaders that any future government would not engage in retribution against the military, the local commanders at military installations in Havana told Machado they could no longer support him. On the same day, August 12, Machado and his cabinet resigned. Machado left for Nassau that night carrying seven bags of gold. General Herrera became the interim president, who quickly turned the presidency over to Carlos Manuel de Céspedes, the son of the hero of Cuba Libre and the favorite of Welles and the U.S. government. Vengeance against the supporters of Machado, the *porristas* and the police was carried out with impunity in the streets of Havana and across the island. It is estimated that 1,000 people were killed and 300 homes were looted on April 12 and 13 in Havana. The ABC hunted down and murdered as many *porristas* as possible by staging neighborhood executions complete with witnesses and drum rolls. In rural areas, wealthy landowners were threatened by workers. Céspedes faced an almost impossible task of trying to restore political order in the midst of the depression. In fact, Welles reported that as late as August 24 the country was still in a state of chaos.

This American-backed deal was not received well by some of the opposition. Céspedes and his cabinet were viewed as nonreformist, made up of individuals perceived to be extremely pro-American and did not have representatives from some of the major groups that had fought against Machado—the radicals from the ABC, the DEU, the CNOC, university professors and former president Menocal and his supporters. Céspedes's refusal to do away with the 1901 constitution, which included the Platt Amendment, provided enough evidence to the opposition groups that he was standing in the way of the more progressive and nationalistic reforms for which they had fought. A devastating hurricane hit the island in early September and foreshadowed the events of the next few days. It was at this point that the "sergeants' revolt" occurred.

The Cuban military was in a difficult situation. It was reluctant to enforce law and order, fearing that the anti-Machado groups would use this as an excuse to restructure and reduce the size of the military. There were increasing demands to purge the military officer corps of its *machadistas*. When upper-level officer vacancies did occur, Céspedes filled them with supporters of former president Menocal rather than with current junior officers. This upset many junior officers who were seeking promotions. They began protecting themselves by demanding that vacancies in the junior officer corps be filled only with graduates of the military academy and the army agreed to their demands in late August. Sergeants would no longer be allowed to fill vacancies at the junior officer level. At Camp Columbia in Havana, the mulatto Sergeant Fulgencio Batista, upset with the order that would restrict the promotions of enlisted men to junior officer positions and a proposed reduction in pay, led a mutiny against the officers and seized control of the camp. Enlisted men at La Cabana joined the mutiny. The sergeants' revolt clearly had racial overtones as a white officer corps tied to a corrupt government was replaced with predominantly nonwhite noncommissioned officers and enlisted personnel.

With the cabinet fearing an attack and Céspedes in Oriente observing the hurricane, the opposition student groups met with Batista and signed the "Proclamation of the Revolutionaries," which called for a restructuring of the political and economic systems of Cuba based on justice and democracy. The students and the military had united to seize control of the destiny of Cuba. On the night of September 4, Céspedes turned over the government to a five-man group that included Professor Grau, who had the support of many students. Ambassador Welles, viewing the ruling group as "frankly communistic," began organizing the opposition groups, including the deposed officer corps. He asked Roosevelt to send naval ships to Cuba. The five-man ruling group dissolved when one of the members of the group promoted Batista to colonel and commander of the army. Batista then met with students from the DEU and created a new government. On September 10, Grau, the students' favorite, became the president of Cuba.

The new president represented the hopes of the nationalistic students, the Generation of 1930, who saw themselves as finally realizing the dreams of José Martí. Grau immediately abrogated the 1901 constitution, demanded that the United States abrogate the Platt Amendment and called for a constitutional convention for April of the next year. He began purging the government of the followers of Machado and met student demands for greater autonomy at the University of Havana. He instituted pro-labor policies consisting of the creation of a department of labor, an eight-hour workday and restrictions on the importation of cheap laborers from the Caribbean. Cuban citizenship became a requirement for all union leadership positions and half of the workforce in industries and commercial enterprises had to be made up of native Cubans. This directly affected Americans, Spaniards, Jamaicans, Haitians and others from the Caribbean who made up some 21 percent of the population in Cuba. Due to labor problems, Grau seized two American-owned sugar mills (Chaparra and Delicias) in December and temporarily took over the American-owned Cuban Electric Company in January 1934. Other initiatives included granting women the right to vote, establishing twelve-week maternity leave to working mothers, mandating employer-provided child care for infants and prohibiting the practice of firing women from their jobs simply because they were married.

These "leftist" actions were not supported by the United States or American businesses in Cuba. Welles recommended that the United States not recognize the new government and continued to encourage opposition groups consisting of the ABC, the deposed officer corps, the old-line Liberal and Conservative political parties, prominent politicians Menocal and Carlos Mendieta and the URC. The officer corps, which had taken up residence in the magnificent Hotel Nacional, continued to refuse to negotiate with Batista. Batista declared the officers to be deserters and brief hostilities broke out on October 2. The officers surrendered although several were massacred during the panic. With this victory and the subsequent victory over an ABC-led revolt on November 8, Batista had strengthened his position as commander and was now able to reshape the officer corps of the Cuban military. In fact, Welles had already come to believe that Batista represented the only authority in Cuba capable of preserving stability and protecting U.S. economic interests. In November, Welles was replaced with Jefferson Caffery who began working with Batista to get a government in Cuba with which the United States could work. Student leader Antonio Guiteras demanded even more social reforms. Grau, the reformer, was caught between the demands of both the right and the left and had no prospect of gaining U.S. support.

By 1933, the standard of living in Cuba was one-fifth what it had been in 1925. Sugar mills were not producing and banditry in the countryside was common. With the *zafra* beginning in December, Batista realized that the United States would never recognize the Grau government. In the middle of the depression, he knew that sugar exports to the United States were crucial to Cuba and, thus, recognition by the United States was essential. In January 1934, Batista informed Grau that the army was no longer able to support him. A general strike on January 17 led Batista to install Mendieta, the U.S. favorite, as president of Cuba the very next day. Five days later, the U.S. government recognized the new Cuban government, although most realized that the real power in Cuba was Batista and the army. To the Generation of 1930, it also became quite clear that for a revolution to succeed in Cuba it would have to take on the United States.

BATISTA AND THE FAILURE OF REFORM

With the belief that the crisis in Cuba was over and that Batista and the military were more than capable of protecting its interests, the United States abrogated the Platt Amendment in May 1934. This was consistent with Roosevelt's Good Neighbor Policy toward Latin America. He declared that the United States would no longer intervene into the internal affairs of the countries of this region. Of course, this only referred to outright military intervention. This policy reflected the growing reality that the United States could exercise as much, if not more influence by manipulating the growing economic dependence of the region as it could through outright military intervention. With the old political institutions largely discredited, the new civilian government of Cuba became more and more militarized over the next few years. The military was used to suppress labor strikes with the support of the United States and the economic elites of the island. As strikes hit the transportation and utility industries, military personnel stepped in to replace the striking workers. In order to prevent the possibility of strikes by government workers, the government made them all military reservists who were under military supervision during any type of political unrest. Utility companies would often only hire people who were military reservists. In the provinces outside of Havana, the military commanders controlled virtually all government functions. The military continued to provide protection for the sugar plantation owners during the *zafra*. These landowners often provided lists of labor leaders and suspected troublemakers to regional military commanders who would arrest them. Provincial and rural civilian authorities were often replaced by members of the military. Mill owners and businesses clearly recognized the military as the real power in Cuba. According to historian Louis A. Pérez Jr., an American consul in Santiago commented that the reach of the Cuban army was so great that it could even control insignificant city jobs such as street sweepers. With its dominance of the political system, corruption within the military increased dramatically. The family members of military personnel received jobs through a massive patronage system. The former sergeants who were now the military elites of Cuba became the primary beneficiaries of this corrupt system.

Opposition to the militarization of the government appeared with students from the Generation of 1930 and national labor organizations. Some students created the Partido Revolucionario Cubano, also known as the Autentico Party. The Autentico Party was led by Grau, who was living in exile in Mexico. Other students believing that only violent methods would lead to success joined the Joven Cuba led by Guiteras. Joven Cuba led an urban underground against Batista similar to the one waged against Machado. Violence reappeared in the streets. In March 1935, a teacher-led movement objecting to poor educational conditions at elementary schools was joined by the Autenticos and national labor organizations. The outcome was a nationwide strike against the corrupt and pervasive military dominance in Cuba. With transportation, utility and hospital workers on strike in Havana and work stoppages on the sugar mills in the countryside, President Mendieta was unable to control the situation. Martial law was declared and the strike was crushed by the military. The repression continued with military firing squads appearing for the first time in Cuban history. Guiteras of the Joven Cuba was killed by the military in May. Many student and labor leaders were exiled. This successful repression further entrenched the military into virtually every part of the Cuban government. Mendieta's government collapsed in late 1935 and Jose Barnet was appointed as president to oversee new elections in 1936.

Miguel Mariano Gómez, son of the former president, was elected president in 1936. He assumed that he had full authority and immediately began appointing his loyal supporters to military and government positions and dismissing individuals who had gained their jobs largely due to the influence of the army and Batista. These actions clashed with Batista, who pressured the congress to impeach Gómez. He was successfully impeached in December. Federico Laredo Bru, the vice president, assumed the presidency. He, just as Mendieta, was merely a figurehead as Batista and the army continued to function as a shadow government. Batista began catering to labor by providing pensions, insurance and a minimum wage. By this time, the new national labor organization, the Cuban Confederation of Labor (Confederacion de Trabajadores de Cuba; CTC), was effectively controlled by the URC and its leader Blas Roca. Batista, who had made overtures to the URC, effectively brought the CTC under the control of the Ministry of Labor. Public works programs were developed in Havana. The government approved a sugar tax that provided funds for a civic-military school system in rural areas with military personnel serving as teachers and schoolmasters. The military directed rural programs that provided healthcare, housing assistance to orphans and support for the elderly. These activities improved life in rural Cuba. They also served to improve the image of the military in these areas as well as increase the popularity of Batista, who had his eyes on the presidency. With the firm entrenchment of the military in the political system, exiled politicians were allowed to return to Cuba and Laredo Bru called for the drafting of a new constitution.

The constitution of 1940 was written by an elected assembly led by the Autenticos. Student representatives of the Generation of 1930, such as Eduardo Chibas and Carlos Prio Socarras, were rewarded with a very progressive document that guaranteed the protection of civil liberties and women's equal rights. It provided for extensive social welfare provisions, paid vacations for workers and minimum-wage guarantees. It also guaranteed the autonomy of the University of Havana. The new constitution represented a New Deal for Cubans. That same year, Batista, with the support of the economic elites of the island and a coalition of parties including the communists, was elected the first president under the new constitution.

The Batista government of 1940–1944 collaborated with the United States during World War II and received increased economic aid for agricultural and public works programs and loans to increase its sugar crop. The United States bought the entire sugar harvest in 1941. Cuba and the United States signed no less that nine military agreements during the war. Most of these allowed the United States to use Cuban military bases. German submarine activity in the Caribbean actually sank several sugar tankers. World sugar shortages worked to Cuba's favor. Increased U.S. demand for manganese from the Bethlehem Steel Mines in Oriente also proved to be a windfall for the Cuban economy. Batista moved to gain the support of the nonmilitary sectors of Cuba. Administrative posts that were under military control such as customs houses, lighthouses and the civic-military rural education project were returned to civilian authorities. These moves upset many in the military who were benefiting from the military dominance that Batista had orchestrated in the 1930s. With Batista's arbitrary dismissal of the police chief in Havana, military officers became anxious. Fearing a military intervention led by army chief Jose Pedraza, the United States intervened by insisting that political stability and the support of Batista were of the utmost importance to it. This demonstration of American support cut short the plot to overthrow Batista. Remarkably, by 1944 Batista had restored civilian control over the government of Cuba. He had won the confidence of the wealthy elite, labor and many other groups. The political process was relatively open as Batista appointed PSP member Carlos Rafael Rodriguez to his cabinet. Corruption and graft was still common throughout the government, as Batista left office in 1944 and moved to Florida. He lived near the headquarters of mafia leader Meyer Lansky, whom he had met and befriended in the 1930s. Batista was now an extremely wealthy man.

Grau, representing the Autentico Party and promising everyone "a pot of gold and an easy chair," was elected president in 1944. It was made very clear to him by Batista that he should not do anything to threaten the Cuban military and, in fact, Grau won the trust of the military with the support of the United States. He expanded professional development programs, raised the pay of the enlisted men and arranged for more Cuban officers to attend U.S. military academies. By the end of 1944, Grau was able to retire more than 200 officers who were associated with the September sergeants' revolt of 1933. Key positions in the military came to be occupied by those loyal to the Autenticos.

Grau benefited from high sugar prices and production in 1946 reached its highest level since the depression. He placed a small tax on sugar that financed public works programs, especially roads. Havana's population expanded dramatically in the 1940s while U.S. investments in light industry in the city also expanded. J. M. Bens Arrarte, a specialist on Cuban architecture, estimated that Grau spent almost $80 million annually on public works projects that built parks, roads, houses, schools and hospitals, roads in Havana's suburbs and upgraded water and sewage systems. These programs provided jobs for the sugar workers in the off-season. Grau encouraged the formation of unions and by the end of his term 30 to 50 percent of the workforce was organized and most of these were in key industries such as sugar, tobacco, textiles, transportation and light manufacturing. Autenticos in the CTC came to collaborate with the communist leadership.

Grau betrayed the revolutionary and nationalistic ideals that he had exhibited in 1933 by presiding over one of the most corrupt governments in the history of Cuba. The lottery, the sinecure system, kickbacks from public works contracts and gambling and outright thefts or misappropriations of public funds were used to enrich government employees and, in particular, Autentico supporters. Because of the low salaries paid to the majority of government employees, corruption permeated every level of government. It became the way of doing business in Cuba. In addition to corruption, violence reappeared in the form of *gangsterismo*.

Gun battles in the streets of Havana, assassinations, kidnappings and violence on the University of Havana campus became common as the remnants of the more violent anti-Machado groups and the Joven Cuba maneuvered to take advantage of the widespread corruption. These pistol-bearing action groups were used by various parties and government officials to intimidate and gain support for their corrupt activities. The Acción Revolucionaria Guiteras (ARG) had ties to trade unions and one of its leaders, Fabio Ruiz, was appointed chief of police of Havana by Grau in return for election support. The Movimiento Socialista Revolucionario had ties to Grau as one of its members, Mario Salabarria, was appointed chief of secret police by Grau. Another group, the Union Insurrecional Revolucionaria, also had ties to the Grau administration as its members sometimes served as bodyguards for the president and Emilio Tro, its leader, was appointed the chief of police Marianao. All of these action groups had ties to students at the university. Campus politics came to be characterized by competition among these gun-toting action groups for the presidency of the FEU and the control of the sale of textbooks and exam papers.

With the Cold War becoming the dominant force in world politics in 1947, the cooperative relationship between the Autenticos and the PSP became strained. Grau and Prio, the minister of labor, moved to eliminate the PSP's control of the national labor federation, the CTC. Two competing leaderships were selected—one communist and the other Autentico. The majority of labor groups on the island were undecided as to which to follow. In July, Prio used force to take the CTC headquarters from Lazaro Pena and the communists. Prio turned it over to the Autentico unionists and by the fall almost all trade unionists had recognized the noncommunist leadership.

The Autentico corruption under Grau was so great that the charismatic Eduardo Chibas, the son of a wealthy family from Guantánamo, former DEU and Autentico Party leader, created his own Ortodoxo Party. Making "honor against money" as his slogan and demanding a Cuba "free from economic imperialism of Wall Street and from the political imperialism of Rome, Berlin or Moscow," he challenged Prio, the Autentico candidate, for the presidency in 1948. Ricardo Nunez Portuondo was the candidate representing the interests of Batista who had returned from Florida. *Gangsterismo* characterized the campaign as Prio openly used the gunmen of the ARG. Prio won the election with Nunez coming in second. Batista was elected to the senate.

Prio benefited from continued high prices of sugar through 1949 and he represented a continuation of the Grau administration with massive corruption and *gangsterismo*. Trying to divert the public's growing dissatisfaction and disillusionment with what was happening, Prio began trying to place the blame on Grau, his predecessor. He also resorted to the time-honored Cuban tradition of massive public works programs with the promise of jobs. In September 1949, he began negotiating a $200 million loan to finance a new aqueduct in Havana and the dredging of the harbor. In a vain attempt to end the violence, Prio exchanged "government jobs" for an end to the violence by placing more than 2,000 members of the action groups under the massive sinecure system within the Ministries of Health, Labor, Interior and Public Works. With the outbreak of the Korean War, the price of sugar remained high in 1950. Evidence of new wealth could be seen in the growing number of new cars and television sets in Havana.

Chibas effectively exposed the massive corruption of the Autenticos and played a major role in undermining their legitimacy. In August during his very popular weekly Sunday night radio broadcast, Chibas shot himself. This event, which has never been fully explained, left the Ortodoxo Party without leadership. The effect was to further erode the legitimacy of the Cuban political system. The Autentico candidate for president was the respectable Carlos Hevia, an engineer who was closely connected to the Bacardi Rum Company. Autentico hopes increased when it was reported that the 1952 sugar production would hit 5.9 million tons with the United States willing to buy more than the normal Cuban quota due to the inability of the Philippines to fill its quota. The Ortodoxos, stunned by the death of Chibas, selected Roberto Agramonte as their candidate, although most believed he could not win. Rumors were rampant of an Autentico-sponsored *golpe*. The third candidate was Batista, who had been using all of his abilities to gain the support of his old followers. It was clear to many that he could not win the election. In December 1951, a group of junior officers gained the support of Batista to plan the overthrow of the discredited Autentico government in Cuba. There was fear among the remaining Batista loyalists in the army that if the Autenticos should win the election they would be purged and would no longer have access to the benefits of military graft and corruption. Batista and his supporters went into action on March 9 and in the early morning hours of March 10, 1952, Prio escaped Cuba by driving his Buick to the Mexican embassy. The *golpe* by Batista marked the end all hope for democracy in Cuba and ushered in a new era that would have unforeseen consequences for Cuba, the United States and the world.

FULGENCIO BATISTA

A clever, fast-thinking, personable and charming mulatto, Fulgencio Batista was born in 1901 in Veguitas, the major port serving the United Fruit Company in northeastern Cuba. He was the son of a sugar worker who had fought with José Maceo (Antonio Maceo's brother) during the Ten Years' War. Batista attended both public and private schools at night while cutting cane during the day. He worked at many odd jobs (water boy at a plantation, timekeeper of a work gang, carpenter and tailor's apprentice, hand boy at a barber shop and brakeman on the railroad) but primarily as a cane cutter until he joined the army in 1921, where he studied law. This background and knowledge of virtually all parts of Cuban society served him well in his ability to manipulate and dominate Cuban politics for almost thirty years. He left the army briefly in 1923 to work as a teacher but reenlisted shortly thereafter. While working as a sergeant stenographer, Batista came to lead the sergeants' revolt, which propelled him into the labyrinth of Cuban politics in the 1930s from which he emerged as the greatest political broker on the island. After he came to power through a *golpe* on March 10, 1952, he appeared on the cover of *Time* magazine in April with the caption: "Cuba's Batista: He Got Past Democracy's Sentries."

NOTES

1. Hugh Thomas, *Cuba; the Pursuit of Freedom* (New York: Harper and Row, 1971), 515.

2. Benjamin Keen and Keith Haynes, *A History of Latin America*, 6th ed. (Boston: Houghton Mifflin, 2000), 434; and Thomas, *Cuba; the Pursuit of Freedom*, 541.

3. Thomas, *Cuba; the Pursuit of Freedom*, 538.

4. Ibid., 539.

5. Ibid., 549–550.

6. Louis A. Pérez Jr., *On Becoming Cuban* (Chapel Hill: University of North Carolina Press, 1999), 167.

7. Thomas F. O'Brien, "The Revolutionary Mission: American Enterprise in Cuba," *American Historical Review* (June 1993): 765–785.

8. Keen and Haynes, *History of Latin America*, 436.

5

The Fall of Batista: 1952 to 1959

Revolutionary struggles are rare throughout history. Successful revolutionary struggles are even more rare and they are the result of many factors that come together in a given place at a given time. Cuba was no different. The stage for the violent upheaval was set by the existence of striking political, economic and social inequalities with more than one-third of the population considered poor and lacking social mobility, coupled with the growth of a frustrated middle class whose rising expectations could no longer be met by a stagnant, sugar-based economy. A corrupt and repressive government supported by the United States had alienated its own people and spurred the growth of a Cuban identity and nationalism divorced from the United States. Yet, with all of this it still took the appearance of a charismatic leader in the right place at the right time to light the fuse and bring all of these ingredients together to make a revolution in Cuba. That leader was Fidel Castro.

BATISTA SEIZES POWER

On March 10, 1952, Fulgencio Batista with the support of the army seized power from President Carlos Prio Socarras in a swift, bloodless and masterful *golpe*. Batista had been encouraged in late 1951 by loyal officers in the military who were not satisfied with the state of affairs in Cuba. In fact, there was little opposition to Batista's seizure of power. Prio and his Autentico Party had lost much of their credibility due to widespread violence, gangsterism (*gangsterismo*) and corruption. The Ortodoxo Party was very effective in rallying public opinion against the Autentico Party by exposing its corruption, but lacked strong leadership after the death of Eduardo Chibas. Many Cubans were ambivalent about Batista's seizure of power. They wanted an end to gang violence and believed his promise of holding elections in 1953.

Batista filled the military ranks with loyalists. He gave military personnel a pay increase, increased the military pensions of senior officers and purchased modern jet fighters from the United States. Navy officials regained control of the customs houses and regional army commanders replaced governors and mayors. He hired 2,000 new national policemen. Batista declared himself loyal to the 1940 constitution but then suspended all constitutional guarantees and the right to strike. He put forward a new constitution in April that enabled him to deny freedom of speech, press and assembly at any time for a forty-five-day period. Political parties were no longer recognized and an eighty-member consultative council with Batista supporters replaced the Cuban Congress. Batista began censoring the newspapers and jailing or exiling those who came to oppose him.

The end of gang violence and the promise of political stability brought Batista support from economic elites such as the Banker's Association, the Association of Land Owners, the Association of Industries, the Association of Sugar Mill Owners and Planters, the cattle industry and local and foreign business owners. The U.S. government recognized the new Cuban government on March 27. A visit by officials of U.S. Steel Company with the promise of investment signaled strong and continued U.S. economic support. U.S. investment in the mining sector increased. Batista started a new public works program that upgraded roads and built a sorely needed water system for Havana. He used bribery, flattery and intimidation to win the support of some labor leaders while continuing the pro-labor policies of the Prio government. The Cuban Confederation of Labor (Confederacion de Trabajadores de Cuba) led by Eusebio Mujal supported the administration. The Popular Socialist Party (Partido Socialista Popular; PSP) initially denounced the *golpe,* but many continued to work in the Ministry of Labor. The Catholic Church hierarchy tolerated the new government.

With the celebration of the fiftieth anniversary of the birth of the Cuban republic, much of the literature and print media lamented the inability of Cuba to live up to the promise of independence and the ideals of José Martí and the other founding fathers. Guilt and pessimism permeated the Cuban people as Batista tightened his control. Several small plots to topple Batista within the military were discovered in late 1952 and early 1953. Opposition to Batista also appeared among the students at the University of Havana and took the form of demonstrations and riots, although they were sporadic and uncoordinated at this time. With increasing repression and censorship of the media, many students came to the conclusion that violence was the only viable means of removing Batista from power. They also realized that overthrowing Batista would lead to a confrontation with the United States.

Fidel Castro had run for the Cuban House of Representatives in 1952 as a member of the Ortodoxo Party. He had been a supporter of Eduardo Chibas, the Ortodoxo leader who had committed suicide during a radio broadcast. When Batista seized power, Castro began organizing a group in Artemisa with the express purpose of toppling Batista. Many in the group had been active in the Ortodoxo Youth Movement. The group included Abel Santamaria, an employee of an American sugar refinery, his sister Haydee Santamaria, Jesus Montane, an accountant for a Cuban branch of General Motors, and Melba Hernandez, a lawyer who would later marry Montane. Santamaria and Montane had published a secret political newsletter entitled *Son Los Mismos.* Most of Castro's followers in 1953 were not university educated, as they were primarily workers and farmers. Only one person in Castro's group was an official member of the PSP.[1]

The plan, which was worked out in Abel Santamaria's office in Havana, was to attack the Moncada Barracks at Santiago and the Bayamo Barracks in the early morning of July 26 during the carnival. It was hoped that the dancing, partying and drinking during the carnival on the previous night would make it difficult for the soldiers to respond effectively to an attack early in the morning. The purpose of the attack was to capture weapons that would enable Castro to arm his movement in the future and spark a popular uprising in Oriente Province that had a long tradition of revolutionary activities. Castro invoked Martí's ideals and Chibas's policies of promising land reform, sugar reform (such as workers having shares in the company profits and strict Cuban ownership of the sugar industry), the nationalization of the utility companies, a pay increase for teachers in rural areas and rent reductions.

The attacks at both the Moncada and Bayamo Barracks were doomed from the very beginning given that Castro's group was outnumbered more than ten to one and poorly armed. Only a few were killed in the actual attack, but sixty-eight were captured, brutally tortured and executed. Thirty-two ended up in prison and another fifty escaped. Castro escaped initially but was later captured by Lieutenant Pedro Sarria, who did not approve of the torture that was taking place at Moncada Barracks. He took Castro to the civil prison in Santiago under the spotlight of the local media. This probably saved Castro from torture and death. Castro was tried in October and acted in his own defense. He gave an impassioned plea ending with the statement, "Sentence me, I don't mind. History will absolve me." The speech would later be smuggled out of his jail cell one sentence at a time on matchbox covers. Later, it would be rewritten and his "History Will Absolve Me" speech was put into a pamphlet and used as an effective propaganda tool. Castro, his brother Raúl and the other conspirators who were not executed were sentenced to prison on the Isle of Pines.

During his prison stay, Castro wrote many letters that gave clues as to the future of the revolution that he would lead. In these letters, he focused on the themes of Martí and Chibas. He emphasized the corruption, greed and repression of the Batista government; the unemployment, illiteracy and healthcare problems of the Cuban people; the need for land reform given the terribly unequal distribution of land; the problems with an economy based primarily on sugar and the dependence of Cuba on the United States. Other letters focused on the use of propaganda and the media as tools of a revolutionary. Finally, reflecting one of Martí's themes, Castro emphasized the need for Cuban unity. He spoke of "the gigantic, heroic enterprise of uniting the Cubans" and the necessity of "uniting in an unbreakable bundle."

In Castro's absence, women assumed much of the leadership of the 26th of July Movement. They included Haydee Santamaria, who was with Castro at Moncada, and Hernandez, who had helped to defend Castro during his trial. They formed contacts with other women's groups opposed to Batista, such as the Association of United Cuban Women and the Women's Martí Civic Front. They also distributed Castro's "History Will Absolve Me" speech in a pamphlet form.

Batista finally agreed to hold elections and stepped down from the presidency on August 14, 1954, so he could campaign to be officially elected as president. He started his campaign by announcing that $350 million in newly issued government bonds would be used for public works projects. He received large sums of money from companies and wealthy Cubans for his campaign. The Autentico candidate, Ramón Grau San Martín, withdrew from the election that was a sham from the very beginning. Batista was elected without any opposition on November 1 and assumed office in February. He claimed that a constitutional government had been restored. Vice President Richard Nixon visited the island and gave the government U.S. support. Believing he was in control and feeling invulnerable, Batista made a fateful decision. He granted a general amnesty to all prisoners. Castro and his comrades walked out of the prison on the Isle of Pines on May 15, 1955.

Castro immediately began attacking Batista in speeches at public meetings and on the radio. He wrote articles for various newspapers, the journal *La Calle* and the magazine *Bohemia.* These came to be censored by Batista. Castro decided, once again, that the use of violence was the only way to topple Batista. Raúl Castro and others left for Mexico to begin preparations for an armed invasion of Cuba. Castro met with those supporters who were to remain on the island. They included not only those from the ill-fated attack at Moncada, such as Haydee Santamaria and Pedro Miret, but also Frank Pais, Celia Sánchez, Faustino Pérez, Armando Hart and Carlos Franqui. These supporters formed the basis for the 26th of July Movement on the island. Castro left for Mexico on July 7, 1955. Enough money was raised to purchase some arms and a farm outside of Mexico City to begin the military training of Castro's group of revolutionaries. Among these revolutionaries was Ernesto "Che" Guevara, a young Argentine doctor who would become second in command and play a major role in Castro's revolution. The Mexican government frequently harassed Castro and his group by seizing their arms and arresting some of them.

Meanwhile, the students at the University of Havana, led by Jose Echeverria, began a more violent campaign against Batista after negotiations with the major opposition parties failed to bring about a political settlement. Police arrested and brutalized many students at anti-Batista rallies in Havana and Santiago in November. Echeverria organized a nationwide student strike. By the end of 1955, Echeverria organized the Revolutionary Directorate, a clandestine student organization whose goal was to topple Batista. Student rioting continued through the early months of 1956 across the island. Batista retaliated with increasing violence. Many students were killed and became instant martyrs.

Dissident officers in the army led by the nationally known and decorated Colonel Ramón Barquin conspired against Batista in April 1956. Barquin represented the young, professional, nonpolitical officers who had come to resent the politicization of the armed forces by Batista. Barquin's supporters represented the best of the Cuban military. Two hundred twenty officers were implicated in the conspiracy and most were tried and thrown in jail. This conspiracy clearly surprised Batista and publicly exposed the open dissension within the Cuban military. Batista became obsessed with loyalty to him as the major requirement of his officers. This increasingly led to the Cuban military coming under the control of political appointees—officers who lacked the professional qualifications that were needed to gain the confidence of the men serving under them.

Echeverria then traveled to Mexico and met with Castro. He agreed to support Castro's invasion with diversionary riots and student demonstrations in Havana. Frank Pais, the leader of the 26th of July Movement's national underground, also traveled to Mexico to work out the details of the invasion. Pais was to organize a general strike and plan for a general uprising that would coincide with Castro's landing in Cuba. Castro and eighty-two companions crowded onto a small yacht named the *Granma* and left Mexico on November 25. The faculty and administrators cancelled classes at the University of Havana while Pais and the 26th of July Movement staged an uprising on November 30 in Oriente

Province by attacking several military installations and engaging in several acts of sabotage, such as derailing trains and cutting down power lines. By the time Castro and his followers landed near Niquero on December 2, the uprising in Oriente had been crushed by Batista's forces. Castro's men made it to a sugar cane field in Alegria de Pio on December 5 where Batista's troops surprised them. Castro and eleven others were the only ones to escape the ambush. With the assistance of some local peasants, the revolutionaries avoided capture for the next several days and made their way into the mountains of the Sierra Maestra. A few days before Christmas, the group cooked two pigs and celebrated the "commencement of the victory of the revolution."

THE STRUGGLE AGAINST BATISTA

On Christmas Eve, the 26th of July Movement encouraged strikes and bombed several facilities in Oriente, causing a blackout in several cities. On New Year's Eve, bombs were exploded in several hotels in Havana and in the city of Santiago. Batista responded with torture and brutality toward anyone associated with the opposition, but the bombings continued. Still, the rebellion was not considered to be a major problem by either Batista or the United States, which continued to support him politically and economically. In fact, it was widely reported that Castro was dead and that his small group of supporters would be captured very shortly.

It was in the Sierra Maestra, the rugged, jungle-covered mountains of southeastern Cuba, that Castro waged his guerrilla war against Batista. It was here that Radio Rebelde began broadcasting the revolutionary propaganda that he would use so successfully. It was here that the legend of Castro started. The hardships suffered by the bearded guerrillas (*los barbudos*), the constant moving from one place to the next to avoid a major confrontation with the Cuban army, the harassment and hit-and-run tactics used by the guerrillas against the army, the support given to Castro by the local peasants and the ability to attract new recruits to the revolutionary group added to the growing heroic image of Castro over the next two years.

With about twenty men, the Fidelistas successfully attacked a small military outpost on January 17 at La Plata and obtained some needed supplies. Even with this, the morale among Castro's small force was low due to the harshness of the mountains, the presence of planes above them and the necessity of dealing with traitors in the group. Castro knew the power of the media and realized that he desperately needed to get his message out to the rest of Cuba and to the world. He arranged for a reporter, Herbert Matthews of the *New York Times*, to come to the Sierra Maestra and interview him. Matthews's interview appeared in the *New York Times* on February 24, complete with pictures of the bearded Castro in his army fatigues. This interview helped to create the legend and mystique of Castro as a hero, a modern-day Robin Hood fighting for justice and resisting oppression. It made him an international figure and all of Cuba finally knew that Castro was alive and well in the Sierra Maestra. Several other writers, journalists, broadcasters and photographers followed Matthews into the mountains to find out about Castro and his guerrillas. By this time, Celia Sánchez, the daughter of a physician in Pilon, Haydee Santamaria and Vilma Espin, the daughter of a wealthy Bacardi Rum Company executive, had joined the guerrillas in the mountains. Castro and his guerrillas also met with leaders of the 26th of July Movement from across the island in late February. Pais promised Castro reinforcements and in March he sent fifty-two new recruits from Oriente to join the Fidelistas in the mountains. Among these recruits was Hubert Matos, a local rice grower, who would later become a guerrilla commander.

In Havana, Echeverria and his Revolutionary Directorate staged a daring attack on Batista's palace. The goal was to assassinate Batista, capture Havana radio and announce the end of the dictatorship. Echeverria and most of the student rebels were killed during the attack. Besides Castro, Echeverria was the most important opposition leader. With his death and the increasing repression and brutality of Batista, all of the opposition now looked to Castro for leadership. Interestingly enough, Cuba's elites, U.S. businessmen and the U.S. government rallied to the support of Batista. World sugar prices were high, U.S. investment was increasing and Batista continued an extensive public works program. The new Havana Hilton opened in April and the next month Batista was recognized as an honorary citizen of Texas.

Castro and his guerrillas captured a military outpost at El Uvero in May. This much needed victory gave the rebels needed weapons, ammunition and supplies, as well as a boost in morale. Castro's guerrillas had come of age and they began to believe they could defeat Batista's army. Knowledge of the mountain terrain gave the guerrillas an advantage over the Cuban army. Repression by Batista's army and local police led peasants to join Castro and rural villages provided invaluable assistance to the guerrillas. On July 30, Pais was trapped in Santiago and shot. A general strike immediately started in the eastern provinces of Cuba.

Throughout 1957 Castro's force in the mountains continued to grow in size and a headquarters was established at La Plata. At the same time, an urban underground in Havana and Santiago waged a brutal, terrorist war against Batista. Several groups including the Civic Resistance, the Revolutionary Directorate and the 26th of July Movement engaged in bombings, kidnappings, assassinations and propaganda distribution. Batista's indiscriminate and brutal retaliation against these groups turned much of the Cuban middle class against him. In September, segments of the navy in Cienfuegos mutinied and captured the naval installation at Cayo Loco. The rebel sailors worked with armed units of the Autentico underground and the 26th of July Movement. Batista was able to put down the rebellion only after extensive troop reinforcements arrived with tanks and aircraft. He then purged the officer corps of the navy. It was also found that some Cuban air force pilots had refused to bomb Cienfuegos during the naval uprising. With the Barquin conspiracy in the army and the navy and air force rebellion in Cienfuegos, it was clear to Batista that he could no longer count on the total support of the armed forces.

By the end of 1957, U.S. ambassador Earl Smith and the American business community wanted an end to the political crisis. The Catholic Church called for the creation of a government of national unity. The war widened when Raúl Castro led rebels to the Sierra de Cristal on northern coast of Oriente to set up a second front in March 1958. A few influential members of the U.S. State Department, including William Wieland, Roy Rubottom and Robert Murphy, were not supportive of Batista and were upset that U.S. arms were being supplied to his repressive regime. On March 13, 1958, the United States suspended a shipment of arms to Cuba. In effect, the United States had put in place an arms embargo. Many Cubans viewed this as a change in U.S. policy and it clearly affected the morale of the Batista government and the armed forces.

A general strike in April failed largely due to the lack of support from the PSP. Batista then launched a major offensive against Castro's guerrillas in May. It consisted of 10,000 to 12,000 men moving into the Sierra Maestra. Naval units bombarded the mountains while planes strafed and bombed areas of suspected guerrilla activity. Batista's offensive had failed by August. Castro captured and turned over 443 prisoners to the International Red Cross. He also gained needed ammunition, guns and tanks from Batista's soldiers. In October and November, Guevara and Camilo Cienfuegos set up additional guerrilla fronts in Las Villas. By this time, desertions and defections from the Cuban army were common. The Fidelistas treated the prisoners with respect, gave medical attention to the wounded and returned soldiers unharmed. The end of the struggle was near as the Catholic Church, the business community and others put pressure on Batista to find a peaceful solution. He held elections in November. With the victory of his self-appointed successor, Andrés Rivero Aguero, through rigged elections, most Cubans came to the conclusion that only violence would bring an end to the Batista government.

Events moved quickly as the guerrillas chalked up one military victory after another over Batista's demoralized troops. Guevara and Cienfuegos set up a front with the guerrillas from the Revolutionary Directorate in the Sierra de Escambray, while Castro and Raúl began to encircle Santiago. On November 30, Castro took Guisa near Bayamo. On December 28, Guevara captured an entire train of Batista's troops while he was advancing on Santa Clara. Santa Clara fell on December 30. In the evening of December 31, Batista was told that Santiago was about to fall to Castro and his guerrillas. At 2:00 A.M. on January 1, 1959, Batista and his closest associates fled to the Dominican Republic. That evening Castro entered Santiago and called for a general strike. The next day Guevara and Cienfuegos entered Havana. The stage was set for Castro's triumphant parade across the island to Havana. A new chapter in the history of Cuba was about to be written.

CUBA ON THE EVE OF THE REVOLUTION

Cuba had changed dramatically since independence, yet in many other ways it had not. The population had doubled to 6.3 million and most Cubans lived in urban areas. There were 21 cities with populations in excess of 25,000 and one-third of all Cubans lived in cities with a population greater than 50,000. Havana and

Marianao, its suburb, approached 1.4 million.[2] Cuba had more television sets per capita than any other country in Latin America and was second only to Venezuela in the number of automobiles per capita. Its average per capita income was the third highest in all of Latin America and the number of telephones per capita was third highest. But these statistics masked the huge gap between the rich and the poor. Cuba was an island of stark contrasts. Havana was the industrial and commercial center, the eastern part of the island was primarily large landed estates dedicated to export-agriculture and cattle and the western part of the island was made up primarily of farmers working small plots of land.

One could see clear distinctions between the urban and the rural areas, Havana and the rest of the island and among social classes. Urban workers were well paid compared to their rural counterparts. The per capita income for urban workers had reached $374, yet for rural workers it was only $91.[3] Almost 87 percent of urban homes had electricity compared to only 9 percent in rural areas.[4] Most rural homes (called *bohios*) were primarily made of palm and wood, lacked running water and bathroom facilities and had earthen floors. Rural dwellers were four times more likely to be illiterate than urban dwellers.[5] Rural unemployment varied with the season—much of it based on the planting and harvesting of sugar. The urban areas, especially Havana, had become magnets that attracted those living in the rural areas to the promise of a better life.

Havana received nearly 75 percent of all investment on the island, excluding the sugar industry. Fifty-two percent of the non-sugar industrial sector was located in Havana. There was one doctor for every 1,000 people on the island, yet more than 50 percent of the doctors lived in Havana. Havana had 60 percent of the dentists, 65 percent of the nurses and veterinarians and 66 percent of the chemists.[6] Cuba's elites and growing middle class lived there. The nightclubs, gambling casinos and hotels of the city were playgrounds for wealthy Cubans and American tourists. On the surface, Havana was rich and prosperous with its world-famous ocean front promenade, the Malecon, its colonial forts, El Morro and La Cabana, its nightclubs, casinos, hotels and its affluent neighborhoods in the western part of the city. Textiles, food processing, cosmetics and the construction industries contributed to the city's economy. The busy port area with its shipyards was surrounded by oil refineries owned by Esso, Shell and Texaco and gas and electric power companies.

At the same time, squatter settlements and shantytowns (*barrios insalubres*), such as Las Yaguas, Llega y Pon and La Cueva del Humo, surrounded Havana and were fed by a constant stream of immigrants from the countryside. The city was not able to provide the necessary services to these shantytowns. The influx of people from the countryside created a surplus labor pool that kept wages low. The vast majority of poor women worked as domestics (cooks, maids and so on) for middle- and upper-class families. Public schools in Havana were scarce and in terrible condition while the private schools catered only to middle- and upper-class residents. This contributed to the lack of social mobility in Havana. The poor had to rely on charities for medical care.

Havana also had a dark, corrupt and sordid side to it. Organized crime from the United States owned or partially owned many of the gambling establishments. Such notable underground figures as Meyer Lansky and Santos Trafficante, who controlled the Sans Souci and the Casino International, were implicated to be part of the behind-the-scenes syndicate that controlled the Riviera, the Tropicana, the Sevilla Biltmore, the Capri Hotel and the Havana Hilton. The casinos regularly paid off corrupt Cuban government officials. In fact, this was an accepted part of doing business. Prostitution was rampant and catered to all social classes as well as tourists and American sailors. Many people in Havana were forced to place a sign on their doors stating, "Don't Bother: Family House," because of the large number of prostitutes who worked out of their own homes.

By Latin American standards, Cuba had a large middle class. Its largest source of income was rental property in the urban areas. In fact, 60 percent of all Cuban families and 75 percent of those in Havana paid rent on their residence.[7] The Cuban middle class of the 1950s was frustrated due to the lack of opportunities afforded it by a stagnant, sugar-based economy and this was especially true of those graduating from the universities. The University of Havana produced nearly 1,200 graduates per year, yet there were few real opportunities for them. Underemployment was the rule, as university graduates worked as clerks in the local Woolworth's Department Stores. In order to meet the rising costs of living, many middle-class women started to work outside the home. This occurred at precisely the same time that employment opportunities were shrinking. There was a surplus of lawyers. Many doctors worked as orderlies to help supplement their incomes. It was very difficult, if not impossible, for the middle class to maintain its standard of living in the 1950s.

Cuba's landed aristocracy had disappeared after the turn of the century and was replaced with large, productive estates with Cuban names but owned primarily by North American companies and absentee landlords. Twenty-eight percent of the largest sugar producers controlled one-fifth of the arable land. Yet, half the land on these estates was idle. Although a few landowning aristocratic families still existed (Calvos, Montalvos, Pedrosos, Agramontes and Betancourt), most wealthy Cubans were in commerce and business and lived in Havana. They joined exclusive social clubs that had come to own much of the Havana waterfront. They sent their children to universities and schools in the United States or to the more prestigious private schools in the city such as Colegio de Belen (where Fidel Castro studied), Colegio de La Salle, Merici Academy, Sagrado Corazon, Ruston and Phillips. The top 10 percent of wage earners accumulated 38.5 percent of all income in Cuba.[8]

The Cuban poor that lived either in the rural areas or in the shantytowns surrounding the urban areas lacked the means of social mobility. Twenty percent of all Cubans were illiterate and this figure was much higher in the rural areas. A smaller percentage of students attended school in the 1950s than in the 1920s. Only 40 percent of school-age children attended school with only 44 percent of children ages six to fourteen and 17 percent of children ages fifteen to nineteen attending.[9] A large percentage of the Cuban poor were Africans and mulattos.

The Cuban economy depended on the export of agricultural products and sugar continued to dominate the economy of Cuba as it had since the late 1800s. The popular saying "without sugar, no country" indicated the importance of sugar to Cuba. More than 80 percent of its foreign earnings were from the export of sugar. Relatively small changes in the price of sugar on the world market dramatically affected the Cuban economy, not to mention natural disasters such as hurricanes. Sugar production took up half of the arable land and a quarter of the labor force. Sugar workers suffered unemployment much of the year because of the seasonal nature of work on the sugar plantations and in the mills. By 1952, it was evident that Cuba was suffering from a stagnant economy.

Per capita income fell by 18 percent between 1952 and 1954. The sugar industry was in need of modernization, as the last sugar mill was built in 1925. Cuba now produced 10 percent of the world's sugar, whereas it had produced 20 percent in the 1920s. In 1957 in Havana, the cost of potatoes increased by 37 percent, black beans by 31 percent and rice by 28 percent. In 1958, the cost of potatoes increased by another 52 percent, black beans by 88 percent and rice by 30 percent. Cubans faced a declining standard of living across the island.[10]

Cuba had become economically dependent on the United States by the turn of the century and by the 1950s that dependence was even greater. Through a quota system, Cuban sugar was guaranteed a market in the United States at above the world market price. In the 1950s, the United States purchased more than half of the sugar produced by Cuba. The United States had invested more than $1 billion in Cuba and owned half of the arable land. In fact, the United States controlled 40 percent of Cuba's sugar production, 90 percent of its utilities and telephones and 50 percent of its railroads.[11] The United States also had interests in mining, oil refineries, rubber by-products, livestock, cement, tourism and a quarter of all bank deposits. Eighty percent of Cuba's imports came from the United States. Foodstuffs amounted to 22 percent of imports.[12] Although most foodstuffs could have been produced locally, U.S. producers pressured Cuba not to produce the foodstuffs locally so as to guarantee a market for its companies.

Not only was Cuba economically dependent on the United States, but also most Cubans had come to identify themselves with the American way of life. The pervasiveness of Americans, American companies and products and American ideas since the turn of the century had left its impact on the island and its people. Baseball had become the Cuban national pastime. Cubans knew of the best American players and many Americans played in Cuba in the off-season. Many Cubans played with American professional teams. The Cuban sense of progress was measured in their ability to purchase American goods, such as televisions, radios, refrigerators and automobiles. They had developed a sense of an entitlement to the American standard of living. They admired American democratic institutions and believed Americans to live up to those democratic ideals. Yet, the economic stagnation of the 1950s forced many Cubans to realize that they would never achieve the American way of life. This, coupled with the realization that Americans would never view Cubans as equals, led to a growing disenchantment with and resentment toward the United States. This was especially true among the 150,000 Cubans, who were typically U.S.-educated, that worked for American companies on the island. By local standards, these Cubans were prosperous. Yet, they were able to see that the Americans on the island did not live up to their stated ideals and standards of fair play and equal treatment. They received firsthand the brunt of American discrimination and racism toward Cubans. Cubans were never in the top-level management, no matter how well they were educated. Cubans, who did the same job as Americans, received lower salaries. Historian Louis A. Pérez Jr. reports that one Cuban, who worked for the Cuban Electric Company as a bilingual clerk, stated his growing resentment, "North American clerks, who knew only English, and often with poor handwriting and performing inferior work, earned much more than the Cubans." Another Cuban engineer who worked for the Owens-Illinois Glass Company stated, "The American engineers got higher salaries," although he and a friend, "carried all weight of the work on their shoulders . . . these were the rules of the game and you had to play it that way."

Batista's *golpe* of 1952 and the U.S. recognition of, indifference to and then support for Batista's repression served to increase the growing divide between Cuba and the United States. Cubans questioned America's commitment to democratic principles. They came to resent the American depiction of Havana in the *Saturday Evening Post* and *Time* as a city of gangsters and sin, the brothel of the Caribbean. They came to recognize that Americans had played just as much, if not an even a greater role as Cubans in the creation of the Havana of 1959. Cuba was searching for its own identity separate from the United States. Nationalism was growing and the United States was its target. The stage was set for Fidel Castro's revolution.

FIDEL CASTRO: THE MAN AND THE MYTH

Castro was born on August 13, 1926, on his father's sugar plantation near Biran on the northern coast of Oriente Province. The U.S. influence in this area of Cuba was pervasive with the United Fruit Company, the Dumois-Nipe Company, the Spanish American Iron Company and the Cuba Railway Company dominating the economy. The U.S. government owned the Nicaro nickel deposits just a few miles down the coast. The vast majority of Cubans lived in poverty while Americans enjoyed their own polo club, swimming pools, schools, stores and hospitals. Angel, Castro's father, was originally from Galicia, Spain. He had fought for the Spaniards and worked for the United Fruit Company before eventually accumulating a hacienda of 10,000 to 23,000 acres of land and employing as many as 500 workers. Castro has never talked much about his father, but evidence indicates that they were neither close nor affectionate. He once referred to his father as "one of those who abuse the powers they wrench from the people with deceitful promises." In an interview with the noted biographer Lee Lockwood, Castro indicated that his father never paid taxes on his land or income and showed his contempt for him by saying that his father "played politics for money." Castro's father died in 1956. His mother was a Cuban Creole whose family was also from Galicia. She protested when the 26th of July Movement burned sugar cane on the family plantation in 1957 and was outraged when the hacienda was nationalized under her son's agrarian reform policies. She and Castro's youngest sister, Juanita, assisted anti-Castro groups in 1962 and 1963. These activities were overlooked by Castro. After his mother died in 1965, Castro arranged for Juanita to go to the United States. She never reconciled with her brother. Castro had seven brothers and sisters, as well as a half brother and sister. The most important of these was Raúl, who was four years younger, and has been with Fidel since the attack on the Moncada Barracks.

At an early age, Castro was sent off to school in Santiago where he stayed with godparents who mistreated him. His first memory of an event that "left a lasting impression" on him concerning the brutal nature of politics in Cuba occurred in Santiago. A group of sailors claimed that some students had said something about them. They followed the students into a nearby building, beat them with the butt of their guns and hauled them to jail. Although not the best student, Castro loved the study of history. He was quite rebellious and at the age of thirteen he tried to organize a strike of sugar workers against his father. In 1942, a tall, heavy and powerfully built Castro attended Colegio de Belen, the prestigious Jesuit preparatory school located in Havana where his best subjects were agriculture, Spanish and history. One day he quarreled with an older and bigger student who beat him until he could not continue. The next day Castro came back for more and was beaten again until the two were separated. Castro came back for more on the third day and again was beaten, but the other boy had had enough and conceded a moral victory to Fidel. Clearly, one of Castro's defining characteristics is that he will not accept defeat. He was a noted debater and voted the best athlete in the school in 1944. The school yearbook noted that he was a true athlete, had won the affection and admiration of all and that he was of "good timber and the actor in him will not be lacking."

He started studying law at the University of Havana in 1945. This period of Castro's life is very controversial and it is difficult to separate myth from reality. Cuban university students had been politicized since the presidency of Machado and the rivalry between the major student groups on campus amounted to *gangsterismo*, with the use of guns, violence and kidnappings being very common. Castro became part of this environment and excelled in it by seeking a student leadership position. He took part in the failed invasion of the Dominican Republic organized by several student groups in 1947. The purpose was to overthrow the dictator Rafael Trujillo. The ships were to set sail from the Bay of Nipe and Castro was in charge of Dominican exiles. At the insistence of the United States, President Grau stopped the invasion and most of the participants ended up being arrested. Castro escaped by swimming across the shark-infested waters of the Bay of Nipe to his father's plantation.

Castro married Mirta Diaz-Balart in 1948. Her father and brother were government officials in the Prio government and never approved of the marriage. Castro's son Fidelito was born in 1948. While Castro was in prison on the Isle of Pines, Mirta was desperate for money. Her brother arranged for her to receive a monthly allowance from the government. When Batista's minister of the interior heard that Castro's wife worked for the Batista government, he published this fact and then dismissed her. Mirta later divorced Castro and remarried. In the 1950s Castro had an affair with Natalia Revuelta. They had one child, Alina Fernandez, who now lives in Spain. During the literacy campaigns of the 1960s Castro met and married Dalia Soto del Valle, a school teacher. They currently live a quiet, comfortable, but austere life in a home in western Havana. They have 5 sons.

These events early in his life shaped Castro's struggle with Batista from the attack on Moncada to prison on the Isle of Pines to the Sierra Maestra to his arrival in Havana in January 1959. They shaped his revolution once he was in power. The athletic and charismatic Castro is mischievous, rebellious, calculating and opportunistic. He is ruthless yet kind. He never accepts defeat—it is only a temporary setback. He is both an idealist and a pragmatist. Castro has a flare for the dramatic and an intuitive sense of the importance of public relations and the use of the media to his advantage. He is somewhat of a loner and rarely confides completely in anyone. He typically learns by trial and error. Castro has a strong sense of the history of Cuba. He saw the need to "overturn the economic status of the nation from top to bottom— that is to say the status of the mass of the people, for it is here that one finds the root of the tragedy [in Cuba]." He saw the pervasive influence and domination of Cuba by the United States. His goal was to carve out a Cuban identity and nationalism separate from the United States—a true Cuban identity. Castro's opportunity arrived in January 1959.

NOTES

1. Hugh Thomas, *Cuba; the Pursuit of Freedom* (New York: Harper and Row, 1971), 826.

2. Ibid., 1094.

3. Roberto Segre, Mario Coyula and Joseph Scarpaci, *Havana* (New York: Wiley, 1997), 88.

4. Ibid., 93.

5. Jaime Suchlicki, *Cuba: From Columbus to Castro*, 2nd ed. (Washington, D.C.: Pergamon-Brassey's, 1986), 136.

6. Thomas, *Cuba; the Pursuit of Freedom*, 1105.

7. Ibid., 1096; Segre, Coyula and Scarpaci, *Havana*, 92.

8. Segre, Coyula and Scarpaci, *Havana*, 88.

9. Thomas, *Cuba; the Pursuit of Freedom*, 1131.

10. Louis A. Pérez Jr., *On Becoming Cuban* (Chapel Hill: University of North Carolina Press, 1999), 453.

11. Segre, Coyula and Scarpaci, *Havana*, 88.

12. Ibid., 89.

6

Revolution and Cold War: 1959 to 1970

When Fidel Castro and his bearded guerrillas triumphantly entered Havana on the evening of January 8, 1959, no one could have predicted the direction of the revolution or that this small island nation of 6.5 million people would become a flash point for the Cold War rivalry between the United States and the Soviet Union. Yet, by the middle of April 1961 the defining themes of the revolution were clearly in place. The charismatic Castro had come to dominate the political scene like no Cuban leader before him. He defied the United States and created the first communist government in the Western Hemisphere, although it clearly reflected his own revolutionary design and imprint. A socialist economy was developed with programs designed specifically to redistribute wealth and address the needs of the poor majority in Cuba. Fueled by the mutual suspicions of the Cold War, the relationship between the United States and Cuba rapidly deteriorated to the point of outright hostilities during the ill-fated attempt by U.S. government–supported Cuban exiles to topple Castro in the Bay of Pigs invasion in April 1961 and, later, the nuclear confrontation in October 1962. Mutually beneficial ties between Cuba and the Soviet Union were established and although the nature of these ties changed over the course of the Cold War, each country used the other to achieve its own national objectives.

THE CRUCIAL YEARS—1959 TO THE BAY OF PIGS

Castro was the man of the hour in January 1959. The major revolutionary groups—the 26th of July Movement, the rebel army and the Civic Resistance (the urban underground)—looked to him for leadership. Middle-class reformers, the Popular Socialist Party (Partido Socialista Popular; PSP), industrialists and nonsugar agricultural interests turned to him. The Cuban people absolutely adored him. This immense popular support gave Castro the power to radicalize the economy and challenge the powerful economic interests on the island, in particular, the sugar industry and major U.S. corporations. Although there would be a struggle within the new government to give the revolution its direction, it was clear to all that Castro would dominate the process.

Manuel Urrutia became the symbolic president of Cuba in January 1959. All of the former Fulgencio Batista supporters in the national, provincial and urban governments were dismissed. Many of Batista's military and civilian leaders were given public show trials. Hundreds were executed and the government confiscated their properties. The congress was dissolved. On February 7, the Fundamental Law of the Republic was passed, which basically gave all political power to the cabinet. Within a week, Prime Minister Miro Cardona resigned in favor of Castro. The cabinet consisted of communists and noncommunists, reformers and revolutionaries. Its initial goals were to diversify the economy, weaken the pervasive U.S. presence and influence in Cuba and reduce the tremendous economic inequality on the island.

Castro promised a revolution, a radical break with the past. Yet, the first reform program of the new government was not radical, in fact, much of it had been proposed in the 1940s: agrarian reform, industrialization and employment expansion. Moderates and noncommunists in the cabinet, such as Columbia University–educated Felipe Pazos and University of Utah–educated Manuel Ray, played a major role in designing the reforms. Popular support for Castro and the rebel army soared with the passage of the initial reforms. Virtually every labor contract was renegotiated from January through April. In March, rents were slashed 30 to 50 percent, but landlords earning less than 150 pesos in rent income per month were excluded. In the urban areas, anyone who owned a vacant lot was forced to sell it either to the state (the National Savings and Housing Institute) or to anyone who wanted to build a house. That same month Castro began a major land redistribution project in Pinar del Río in which he personally signed over the land to peasants.[1] Tariffs were increased to protect local industries from foreign competition.

On May 17, 1959, the cabinet passed the First Agrarian Reform Law. The law was based primarily on Article 90 of the 1940 constitution and created the National Institute for Agrarian Reform (Instituto Nacional de Reforma Agraria; INRA). It placed a 1,000-acre limit on land holdings. All land beyond the limit was claimed by the government and controlled by the INRA. Expropriated land was either turned into cooperatives to be run by the INRA or distributed to individuals in sixty-seven-acre plots. Sharecroppers and renters had first claim to the expropriated land. Owners were paid for their losses with twenty-year state bonds at 4.5 percent interest. This land limit did not apply to the cattle ranches and the sugar and rice plantations whose yields were greater than 50 percent of the national average. In these cases, the limit on land holdings was set at 3,333 acres. Thus, the law applied only to approximately 10 percent of all the farms, plantations or ranches in Cuba but amounted to 40 percent of the land.[2] Foreign companies could own more land than the limit if the government deemed it was in the national interest. Sugar mill owners could no longer manage the sugar plantations unless all their shares were registered and owned by Cubans. Land could only be purchased by Cubans. The rebel army, which carried out many of the expropriations, the INRA and the National Federation of Sugar Workers (Federacíon Nacional de Trabajadores Azucareros) became the primary institutions that promoted and protected the interests of rural workers under the revolutionary government.

Tax policies were altered to favor Cuban over foreign and primarily U.S. investments, nonsugar over sugar sectors of the economy, small over large businesses and the provinces over Havana. An ad valorem surcharge of 30 to 100 percent was placed on all imported luxury items. The smaller sugar mills and rice growers were given larger quotas for export. As a backlash to the tremendous corruption of the Batista era, stealing from the government became a capital crime. The rampant sinecures system came to an end. Prostitution and gambling became illegal. Even the traditional Cuban practice of cockfighting was declared illegal.

Relations with the United States began to deteriorate rather quickly. The U.S. government opposed the summary trials and executions of Batista supporters largely due to the absence of established legal guarantees and due process. U.S. corporations and businesses opposed the wage increases and labor and land reforms. This resistance inflamed popular opinion against the United States. The seizure of the U.S.-owned Cuban Telephone Company in March 1959 became a symbol of defiance and stoked the passions of nationalism among the Cuban people. The May agrarian reforms contributed to U.S. suspicions of Castro and his revolution. It led to further U.S. opposition because many powerful U.S. interests lost land to the Cuban government and argued that they did not receive adequate compensation. This included the United Fruit Company, the Pingree Ranch and the King Ranch of Texas that had influential ties to powerful people in the U.S. government.[3]

Castro visited the United States in April and even though Cuba needed economic aid, he did not ask for it. He did not want to become another Cuban leader who would discard his revolutionary principles, bow down and become dependent on the United States. After this visit, Vice President Richard Nixon, the State Department and the Central Intelligence Agency (CIA) came to the conclusion that the United States could not have friendly relations with Cuba and efforts to overthrow the revolutionary government were supported and developed. For the next year, Castro and his rebel army fought counterrevolutionary groups and Miami-based Cuban exiles who used air bases in southern Florida to engage in assassination attempts, provide arms to counterrevolutionary groups, burn crops, bomb sugar mills and attack ships bound for Cuba. The U.S. failure to disavow these groups and prevent their activities was enough evidence for Castro to assert U.S. complicity in these actions. In fact, the CIA developed at least eight different plans designed to assassinate Castro over the next five years.

Opposition to the agrarian reforms within Cuba began to appear among various groups. Sugar mill owners and cattle ranchers started a media campaign against the agrarian reform law. The media campaign used the imagery of a watermelon with the idea that the deeper you cut it (the Cuban government) the more red (communist) it becomes. Sugar mill owners, cane growers, rice plantation owners and industrialists opposed the wage increases for workers. Refusing to meet with union representatives, challenging the legality of the unions, cutting back on the number of employees, limiting worker access to credit and engaging in lockouts were tactics used to fight the wage increases that workers demanded. The Labor Ministry mediated more than 5,000 labor-management disputes in early 1959. These mediations were generally settled in favor of the demands of labor. Wage increases averaged 14.3 percent in 1959.[4]

Opposition began to appear within the ranks of the revolutionary leadership. This struggle pitted the noncommunists against the communists. The PSP did not play a major role in the revolution and, in fact, had condemned Castro's attack on the barracks at Moncada and had not become part of the Batista opposition until late 1958 when the final outcome of the struggle was evident. The initial agrarian reforms and nationalizations of foreign industries were made without consulting or informing the PSP and the initial reforms were more radical than PSP proposals. Yet, Castro saw several advantages in using the PSP. It was well organized and could help control the labor movement in Cuba. Interestingly enough, Batista had used the party in the very same way. At the same time, Castro could purge the party of those whose primary loyalty was not to him. Finally, the PSP had ties to the Soviet Union and Castro knew that only the Soviet Union could possibly deter a U.S. attack or action against Cuba similar to what had happened in Guatemala in 1954.

Vocal opposition to the perceived growing communist influence over the new government came from President Urrutia, who was forced to resign in July, and Pedro Diaz Lanz, the head of the Cuban air force and who defected to the United States in June where the U.S. Senate promptly gave him a public forum to tell how the communists were taking over the island. Hubert Matos, the commander of the rebel army in Camagüey Province, also expressed his concerns and opposition to the communists. Camagüey Province was the heart of the counterrevolutionary forces in Cuba. North American companies such as the King Ranch of Texas and the Manati Sugar Company had lost hundreds of thousands of acres of land and many of the more famous Cuban families, such as the Betancourts and the Agramontes, had their estates seized under the new agrarian reform. Matos, a former teacher who had fought with Castro in the Sierra Maestra, had publicly spoken against growing communist influence in the government in June. He resigned when Raúl Castro was named minister of the armed forces in October. Raúl, along with Ernesto "Che" Guevara, were already known for their revolutionary and procommunist beliefs although neither were members of the PSP. Matos was tried for "uncertain, anti-patriotic and anti-revolutionary" behavior and sentenced to twenty years in jail.

Seeing increased divisions within the leadership of the revolution, fearing a repeat of the failed revolution of 1933 and expecting U.S. opposition and interference, Castro began to centralize the revolutionary power structure and emphasize loyalty, unity and survival. Loyalty to Castro became the primary criteria for all future appointments. Revolutionary unity was defined as opposition to the United States and the Cuban elite, meaning the economic class with its historic ties to the United States. Unity also meant that the members of the PSP were to be included in the revolution. The anticommunist resistance in Cuba had come to be more preoccupied and concerned with the future role of the PSP in the government than with the revolutionary goals of ending U.S. dominance, reducing the economic inequality and meeting the needs of the poor majority on the island. Marifeli Pérez-Stable, a noted scholar on Cuba, argues that the controversy over communist influence in Cuba from 1959 to 1961 masked a "repudiation of radical change." The anticommunists were moderates, not revolutionaries, and Castro swept them away. With the moderates gone and the revolutionary leadership unified, the U.S. hope of controlling the revolution faded. It is ironic that the U.S. opposition to the initial economic reforms helped to undermine the legitimacy of the moderates in the revolutionary government and paved the way for Castro to purge them and radicalize the economy—the very thing the U.S. did not want to happen.

Castro began making more of the decisions. There were no more than two cabinet meetings held between October and March 1960. Several moderates in the cabinet—Manuel Ray, Faustino Pérez and Felipe Pazos—resigned. These people were well respected in the United States, in particular, Pazos, who also took with him many of his best technical advisers. These resignations left a shortage of skilled and technically competent administrators and planners in the new government. This clearly played a role in the turn to assistance from Eastern Europe and the Soviet Union. With the resignation of these moderates, U.S. ambassador to Cuba Phillip Bonsul came to the conclusion that the United States would not be able to reach an understanding with the new Cuban government. Survival for revolutionary Cuba during the Cold War meant developing closer ties to the Soviet Union.

In November and December, new laws were passed against foreign corporations. Foreign oil companies had to pay 60 percent of their earnings to the government. Lands from Bethlehem Steel and International Harvester were seized. More lands from the cattle ranches were also seized. It was the arrival of Soviet deputy premier Anastas Mikoyan in February 1960 that confirmed the suspicions of many in the United States that the Cuban revolution was clearly communist. The Soviet Union and Cuba signed a five-year trade agreement in which Cuba would deliver 1 million tons of sugar annually in exchange for Soviet crude oil and the Soviets extended $100 million in credits to Cuba so it could purchase industrial equipment. On March 4, 1960, the ship *La Courbre*, loaded with weapons acquired in France, exploded in Havana Harbor. Castro blamed the CIA and gave a defiant anti-American speech that day in which he ended with what would become the most important slogan of the revolution, *"patria o muerte!"* ("fatherland or death"). Two weeks later, President Dwight Eisenhower approved the development of a covert operation designed to topple the Castro government.

By this time, the United States and Cuba were on a spiraling path of mutual fear and hostility toward an inevitable conflict and there was little possibility of accommodation. Events began to take on a life of their own. In May, Castro announced there would be no elections. He indicated that the Cuban people had already spoken. Given his tremendous popular support, there is no doubt that if elections had been held he would have easily won. The U.S. House of Representatives approved a bill that would allow President Eisenhower to cut foreign sugar quotas at his discretion in June. Under instructions from the Eisenhower administration, Texaco, Shell and Standard Oil refused to refine Soviet crude oil. On June 28, the Cuban government nationalized the foreign oil companies. In July, President Eisenhower cancelled the remainder of the Cuban sugar quota for the year. It should be remembered that the United States purchased 40 to 60 percent of its sugar from

Cuba under a quota system with fixed amounts and guaranteed prices above the world market price. Economic survival required Cuba to sell the remaining sugar that normally was sold to the United States. The Soviet Union agreed to purchase the sugar.

All U.S. businesses such as Sears and Roebuck and Coca-Cola, as well as all sugar mills, petroleum refineries, public utilities, tire plants, ranches and banks were nationalized in August. This also included the U.S. government–owned nickel deposits at Moa Bay. The Eisenhower administration allotted $13 million to provide guerrilla warfare training to 400 to 500 Cuban exiles in Guatemala. The United States pressured the Organization of American States (OAS) to rebuke Cuba in September and, not surprisingly, Cuba strengthened its ties with the Soviet Union and Eastern Europe. Fearing a U.S.-led intervention, Castro organized the Committees for the Defense of the Revolution (CDRs). These local organizations served not only to mobilize the population in support of the government, but also to report any activities against the government. The next month the Cuban government nationalized all industry and commerce and the United States announced an embargo of its exports to Cuba. In late October, a Guatemalan newspaper reported that the United States was training Cuban exiles in that country for an invasion of Cuba. By November there were more than 1,000 Cuban exiles being trained in Guatemala. In December, China agreed to purchase 1 million tons of Cuban sugar and the Soviet Union agreed to purchase 2.7 million tons the following year. Nikita Khrushchev, the Soviet leader, expressed a willingness to defend Cuba from "unprovoked aggressions." By the end of 1960, the Cuban state controlled the primary means of economic production on the island. Cuban capitalism had come to an end and its ties with the communist world were expanding.

The Cuban economy performed quite well in 1959 and 1960. It grew at almost 10 percent a year and the sugar output of 6.2 million tons per year was greater than the average for the years 1950 through 1958. A trade surplus existed by the end of 1960. Wealth had been redistributed with 15 percent of the national income shifting from property owners to wage earners by the middle of 1960.[5] Housing and roads in rural areas were improved. A great sense of optimism among the revolutionary leaders and the Cuban people led to an expectation that the economic goals of reducing

Cuba's dependence on sugar and developing an industrial base for the island would prove to be successful.

The 1961 New Year's Day parade in Havana exhibited Soviet tanks and other weapons. Later that month, President Eisenhower severed diplomatic relations with Cuba when Castro demanded that the United States reduce the size of its embassy staff to eleven, the same size of the Cuban staff at its embassy in Washington, D.C. The incoming U.S. president, John Kennedy, and his advisers were anxious to prove to the world their anticommunist credentials and Cuba was their first target.

THE BAY OF PIGS—CONSOLIDATION OF CASTRO'S POWER

The Bay of Pigs invasion (Playa Girón) in April 1961 represents the pivotal event in the early years of the Cuban revolution. It allowed Castro to consolidate his power and eliminate virtually all his opposition on the island. It gave Castro and the people of Cuba proof that the ultimate goal of the United States was to destroy the Cuban revolution. It convinced a reluctant Soviet Union that a relationship with Cuba could be very beneficial and entailed little risk. Finally, it led to the decision to place nuclear missiles on Cuban soil.

President Kennedy and his advisers inherited the plan for the invasion of Cuba by U.S.-trained Cuban exiles. On April 14, Cuban exiles who had been training in Guatemala boarded ships in Nicaragua and sailed for Cuba. Luis Somoza, the president of Nicaragua, encouraged and asked them to bring him back some of the hair from Castro's beard. On the morning of April 15, a group of B-26 bombers based in Nicaragua attacked key airfields in Cuba. The military damage was insignificant but it prompted Castro to move against his opponents on the island. All dissidents, both real and imagined, including all bishops, many journalists, the vast majority of the urban underground resistance and most of the CIA's 2,500 agents and their 20,000 suspected sympathizers were rounded up and thrown in jail. Castro used the air attacks to mobilize the Cuban public against the United States, concluding a speech in Havana with the phrase *"patria o muerte, venceremos!"* ("fatherland or death, we will conquer!"). Castro received news of the landing of the invasion force at the Bay of Pigs at 3:15 A.M. on April 17. The towns near the Bay of Pigs had been the recipients of many of the initial benefits of the revolution—new roads and tourist centers had been built, a literacy campaign was in progress and the standard of living had increased since 1959. It was an unlikely place to start a counterrevolution against Castro. Cuban forces reacted quickly to the invasion. Two Cuban T-33 jet trainers and a B-26 bomber attacked the landing forces, sunk two ships and chased away the supply ships. Khrushchev threatened Kennedy: "The government of the United States can still prevent the flames of war from spreading into a conflagration which it will be impossible to cope . . . any so called 'small war' can produce a chain reaction in all parts of the world."[6] Kennedy hesitated to authorize air strikes from the USS *Essex* to support the invasion. Eventually, Castro captured 1,180 of the 1,297 who had landed.

It was the perfect victory for Castro. His often-predicted invasion by the United States had finally occurred. The Cubans had won a victory against the United States. The United States and its indecisive young president were humiliated by world public opinion. Castro's popularity among the Cuban people skyrocketed. He was able to enlist 100,000 people in a massive, nationwide literacy campaign. Thousands of urban residents volunteered to cut sugar cane. More than 300,000 local militias and 800,000 CDRs were developed to defend the island against future U.S. invasions. Housewives volunteered for the militias and the CDRs. Castro strengthened and consolidated his control over the political system and destroyed almost all of his opposition on the island. After the invasion, Castro declared the socialist nature of his revolution an obvious attempt to encourage the Soviet Union to develop closer ties to Cuba. The United States with a slim majority suspended Cuba from the OAS in early 1962 and began pressuring its allies to end all trade and commerce with the island.

THE MISSILE CRISIS

The Soviet Union had initially been cautious in its relationship with Cuba. Its experience with revolutionary regimes that had come to power without its support indicated that these governments often pursued independent policies and were, at best, difficult to control. The Soviet Union was more concerned with promoting peaceful coexistence with the United States and gaining concessions in Berlin rather than with events in an area of the world that the United States had traditionally controlled and held an overwhelming strategic and military advantage. Yet, several factors led to the decision to place nuclear missiles in Cuba. The growing competition with China in winning the hearts and minds of revolutionaries in the developing world led the Soviet Union to tolerate and warm-up to revolutionary leaders like Castro. It was the failed Bay of Pigs invasion by the United States that finally convinced the Soviet Union to take a chance in developing closer relations with Cuba. It appeared that the revolutionary government in Cuba now had a chance to succeed given that there was virtually no opposition left on the island. It convinced Khrushchev that the young U.S. president was weak and indecisive and lacked resolve. The Soviet Union believed that world condemnation of the failed invasion would make it difficult for the United States to use force against Castro, at least temporarily. It was seen as a window of opportunity to alter the nuclear balance of power that was in favor of the United States, to win concessions from the United States over issues in Berlin and to deter a future U.S. invasion of Cuba. A closer relationship with Cuba would enable the Soviet Union to achieve these goals.

The Soviet Union increased its military aid to the island. This included aircraft that were capable of delivering nuclear bombs throughout the hemisphere. Even though the Cubans had not requested them, the Soviets began installing medium-range nuclear missiles in Cuba in October 1962. The Cubans had urged them to announce to the world that they were placing missiles in Cuba but the Soviets decided to install them in secrecy. Following the discovery of the missiles, the United States put in place a naval blockade (the United States referred to it as a quarantine because a blockade is an act of war in international law) around the island. The Cubans fully expected a U.S. invasion and air attack. They expected to lose the initial battles and retreat to the mountains to wage a prolonged guerrilla war against the United States. They were ready to fight to the death and thought that the Soviet soldiers would fight and die with them. There was the expectation that if the United States used nuclear weapons against Cuba or was about to overwhelm the island that the Soviets would use the nuclear weapons against the United States.

The agreement between Kennedy and Khrushchev to remove the missiles from Cuba in exchange for a pledge by the United States not to invade the island stunned and humiliated the Cubans. The reality is that Castro and the Cubans were pawns during the missile crisis. Neither the Soviet Union nor the United States consulted with them. Castro heard about the agreement to end the crisis on the radio. The Cubans were angry at the Soviets. In response, Castro set forth several demands that had to be met before he considered the crisis to be over. He called for an end to the U.S. economic embargo of the island, an end to all subversive activities of the United States, an end to U.S. support of Cuban exiles attempting to overthrow its government, respect for Cuban territory and airspace and the return of Guantánamo Bay to Cuba. These demands were ignored by the United States and still are today. The Cubans felt betrayed by the Soviets but there was nothing they could do to stop the removal of the missiles. Relations between the Soviets and Cuba would be strained until August 1968 with the Soviet invasion of Czechoslovakia.

THE NEW SOCIALIST MAN AND THE RADICAL EXPERIMENT

Nearly 250,000 Cubans had fled the island between 1959 and October 1962. Almost all were members of the upper and middle classes and this contributed to the "brain drain" and the lack of qualified personnel to help with the development of the country. Still, there was much optimism about the economic future of Cuba in 1960 and the revolutionary leadership embarked on a strategy designed to reduce the island's dependence on sugar. This was to be achieved through rapid industrialization and the diversification of agriculture. The focus of rapid industrialization was to be in the areas of metallurgy, transportation equipment, chemical products, machinery and sugar cane by-products. All of this required imported technologies and materials. Sugar exports were to provide the necessary funds to purchase the needed imports.

By the spring of 1961, more than 33,000 peasants had become owners of land that they had previously worked as tenants, share-croppers or squatters. There were more than 266 state-run farms. More than 600 sugar cane cooperatives had been created.[7] Problems appeared when sugar output declined sharply in 1962 and 1963. The decline was largely due to mismanagement and the lack of skilled managers. Managers were often farmers with little or no experience in large-scale agriculture. Some were selected largely for political reasons. Cuban workers were simply not used to making decisions and taking the individual initiatives that were required for a cooperative to be successful. Other factors that contributed to the decline in sugar output included a reduction in the amount of land used to grow cane, a failure to replant much of the cane in 1960 and 1961, a rural labor shortage and a prolonged drought in 1961. Just when Cuba needed sugar exports the most to finance its industrialization process, the sugar sector was not able to deliver. There is no doubt that the U.S. embargo played a role in this failure as well. Diversification of agriculture did not meet the growing domestic demand for food (largely due to the downward redistribution of income) and did not generate enough exports to make up for the sugar shortage.[8] Rationing of food began in 1962. The trade and balance of payments deficits ballooned. The lack of skilled personnel contributed to the chaotic and improvised nature of central planning in the Ministry of Industry. The attempt to achieve rapid industrialization failed.

Recognizing that industrialization depended on foreign exchange or capital that only the sugar sector could provide, the revolutionary government adopted a new strategy of development in 1964. This strategy focused on sugar and agriculture. Increasing sugar production for export, the diversification of agriculture and the focus on agricultural support industries became the model for national economic growth. The symbolic goal of this strategy was to be able to produce a massive 10-million-ton sugar harvest in 1970. In order to accomplish this, the state would have to direct the majority of its resources, labor and capital into the production of sugar.

This radical experiment had both internal and external components, as well as both practical and ideological motives. Within Cuba, Castro used his immense popularity and charisma to mobilize the passions and will of the people toward the creation of a "new socialist man." The new socialist man was to be committed to an egalitarian society and place the needs of community before himself. Laborers were to work for the good of society rather than personal gain. They were to work hard out of a moral commitment to the building of a socialist community. Labor unions under the Cuban Confederation of Labor (Confederacion de Trabajadores de Cuba; CTC) became the primary vehicle to promote the new socialist man with its emphasis on moral incentives. Nonmaterial incentives, such as being recognized as a vanguard worker—those who had met the requirements of the so-called new socialist man according to CTC officials—were to compensate for overtime and volunteer work. Urban residents were encouraged to volunteer to work in seasonal agricultural activities such as cutting sugar cane. In support of this commitment to an egalitarian society, the government provided access to social services free of charge. Healthcare, education, day care, social security and much housing were provided free to all Cubans.

By 1964, nearly 63 percent of the cultivated land was controlled by the state.[9] The remaining private farmers had to sell their goods to the state at low prices and volunteer to work on the state farms. Private farmers were encouraged to form their own credit and service cooperatives. In the spring of 1968, the remaining sector yet to be nationalized by the state—small retail businesses, such as food and service shops—came under state control. About 25 percent of the business owners in Havana who had their businesses nationalized went to work in agriculture.[10] Rationing of basic food guaranteed equality, although it did so in the middle of austere economic conditions. Thus, by controlling most of the cultivated land in the country, controlling the output on the remaining private farms, eliminating most private property, using *La Libreta* (the ration book), decreasing the wages for all except the poorest paid Cubans between 1966 and 1970, guaranteeing employment and providing free healthcare, education and social security to all, the Cuban government created the most egalitarian distribution of income in all of Latin America. These policies also allowed the government to increase its revenue and resources to address the balance of payments deficit and to channel investment and more laborers into sugar production. In fact, gross investment by the government increased from 16 percent of the national product in 1962 to 25 percent of the national product in 1967.[11]

The radical experiment also consisted of the campaign against bureaucracy. The goal was to improve administrative efficiency in the government, trade unions and other organizations by streamlining them. This, of course, would also increase the labor pool available to work in agriculture. The number of full-time administrators or bureaucrats in these organizations was reduced dramatically. Under the antibureaucracy campaign, the number of full-time union administrators in the CTC was reduced by 53 percent.[12] By 1965, Castro reorganized the PSP into the Communist Party of Cuba (Partido Comunista de Cuba; PCC) and had purged it of old-line Soviet communists, such as Anibel Escalante, who were less than loyal to him. In effect, he had merged the 26th of July Movement, the PSP and other revolutionary groups into a party that could be used as an instrument of his personal power.

The new socialist man never materialized during the radical experiment. The victories and euphoria of the early years of the revolution were replaced with hard work and austerity. Due to the provision of free education, healthcare, social security, day care and housing, worker wages were almost meaningless. Yet, appeals to socialist ideals failed to motivate workers. Membership in unions declined to the point that less than 20 percent of the workers were members and these were primarily the vanguard workers.[13] Most of the workers were demoralized and resented the low pay, the long hours of work and the lack of material incentives. They resented the back-breaking volunteer work in the sugar cane fields. Resistance took the form of foot-dragging and high absenteeism. This resistance, coupled with a lack of motivation, adversely affected the economic production of the state. Black market activity increased, with the private farmers often supplying the goods that were unavailable through the rationing system. Many private farmers became relatively wealthy. Even the growth in the number of PCC members was primarily from members of the military and government rather than average citizens. Perhaps the most successful organization during the radical experiment was the Federation of Cuban Women (Federacíon de Mujeres Cubanas). It was successful in increasing its membership to 1.3 million, managing day care centers across the island, educating rural women in healthcare and personal hygiene and increasing the female percentage of the labor force to 18.3 percent in 1970.[14] The campaign against bureaucracy simply made economic planning more difficult and contributed to the chaos in the economy by the end of 1970.

Even though Cuba failed to meet the stated goal of 10 million tons of sugar in 1970, it did produce a record crop of 8.5 million tons. Yet, the Cuban economy was in shambles. Nonsugar agriculture and state industry suffered due to neglect and the vast amount of resources that had been redirected toward the production of sugar. In 1968, the world market price of sugar was below Cuban production costs and in 1970 it was less than half of what it had been in 1963. The Soviet Union would only purchase, at the most, 56 percent of the total Cuban sugar crop. Cuba was its own worst enemy. By increasing the world supply of sugar, its price remained depressed. During the radical experiment, sugar had not provided the necessary resources to diversify the economy. In fact, Cuba was as dependent as ever on one crop: sugar.

The external component of the radical experiment focused on the support of revolutionary groups throughout Latin America. The goal, in the words of Guevara, was to create "two, three, many Vietnams." This issue exacerbated the already strained relationship between Cuba and the Soviet Union. The Soviet Union did not agree with Castro's efforts to promote violent revolution in Latin America. Castro believed that the Cuban revolution could be duplicated whereas the Soviets preferred the peaceful road to power via the traditional communist parties in the region. He denounced these parties for their lack of support for guerrilla movements in the region and chided the Soviet Union for its continued recognition of Latin American governments that were hostile to Cuba. Castro and the PCC refused to recognize the leadership of the Soviet Union and emphasized Cuba's right to develop its own foreign policy initiatives concerning revolutionary activities.

Venezuela with its vast oil reserves was a perfect target for an oil-hungry Cuba that was forced to rely on a less than dependable and faraway Soviet Union. Castro began to provide support to revolutionaries and urban terrorists in Venezuela in 1963. He hosted revolutionary leaders from across the world in Havana in 1966 and called for a continent-wide guerrilla struggle led by Cuba. Cuba provided training, arms and funding for revolutionaries throughout region. It is important to remember that this was taking place at the same time that most of Latin America had come under the control of repressive military governments and right-wing dictators who used Cold War anticommunism to gain support and aid from the United States. The United States was more than willing to overlook the repressive nature of these governments and provide military training and support for them in their struggle against these revolutionary groups. In the end, Cuba's support for revolutionaries failed to bring about victory. Revolutionary groups supported by Cuba could neither gain the support of the majority of the population, nor could they escape the military repression directed toward them. With the death of Guevara in the mountains of Bolivia in October 1967, it was clear that Cuba's revolution would not be duplicated in Latin America. The external component of the radical experiment had failed.

CHANGE IN DOMESTIC AND FOREIGN POLICIES

In August 1968, the Soviet Union invaded Czechoslovakia and crushed the attempt at liberalization. Castro spoke in support of the Soviet invasion in an attempt to create a closer, more cooperative relationship between the two countries. He began to show greater solidarity with the Soviet Union. He reversed a PCC decision and allowed a Cuban representative to attend, as an observer, the World Conference of Communist Parties held in the Soviet Union in 1969. The purpose of the conference was to show solidarity against the Chinese Communists. The Soviet navy began to call at Cuban ports, while top-ranking Soviet officials visited Cuba. Castro and his brother Raúl visited the Soviet Union and Eastern Europe for extended periods of time. Several factors led to this change in the relationship between Cuba and the Soviet Union. The death of Guevara in Bolivia in 1967 ended Castro's dream of Cuban-led revolutions throughout Latin America. The Soviet Union had opposed Cuba's revolutionary policies in Latin America and this event removed a major area of disagreement between them. Poor sugar harvests in 1967 and 1968 had increased Cuba's need for Soviet economic aid. The Soviet Union announced a delay in petroleum shipments in January 1968. The island required petroleum and this announcement reminded the Cubans of their dependence on the Soviet Union. The presidential election of Nixon in 1968 also led Castro to a closer and more cooperative relationship with the Soviet Union. Castro saw Nixon as one of the chief architects of the Bay of Pigs invasion and believed that the new U.S. president would turn against Cuba. These factors, coupled with the failed economic strategy in 1970, set the stage for a change in both the domestic and foreign policies of Cuba.

NOTES

1. Hugh Thomas, *Cuba; the Pursuit of Freedom* (New York: Harper and Row, 1971), 1201.

2. Ibid., 1215–1216.

3. Ibid., 1223.

4. Marifeli Pérez-Stable, *The Cuban Revolution* (New York: Oxford University Press, 1999), 68.

5. Ibid., 85.

6. Jaime Suchlicki, *Cuba: From Columbus to Castro,* 2nd ed. (Washington, D.C.: Pergamon-Brassey's, 1986), 165.

7. Thomas, *Cuba; the Pursuit of Freedom*, 1323–1324, 1326.

8. Pérez-Stable, *Cuban Revolution*, 85.

9. Susan Eva Eckstein, *Back from the Future* (Princeton, N.J.: Princeton University Press, 1994), 33.

10. Ibid., 34.

11. Ibid., 38.

12. Pérez-Stable, *Cuban Revolution*, 114.

13. Eckstein, *Back from the Future*, 35.

14. Pérez-Stable, *Cuban Revolution*, 116.

7

Economic Change, Institutionalization and Cold War: 1970 to the End of the Cold War

Revolutionary idealism, spirit, excitement and fervor eventually give way to the realities of everyday living. According to Marifeli Pérez-Stable, the 1960s' radical experiment was born of this revolutionary idealism as well as the concept of revolutionary social justice, the charisma of Fidel Castro, the challenge and hostility of the United States and the growth of Cuban nationalism. After the failure of the radical experiment and the move to closer relations with the Soviet Union, the realities of everyday living in a revolutionary socialist society became evident. Cuba was forced to turn to a more pragmatic strategy of development. From 1970 to the mid-1980s, the Cuban revolution moved to adopt a more institutionalized model of socialism somewhat closer to that in the Soviet Union and Eastern Europe. Yet, it was clear that Cuba under Castro could never imitate this model. The attempt to institutionalize or formalize the role of the Communist Party of Cuba (Partido Comunista de Cuba; PCC) in society could never be complete as long as Castro ruled in such a personal manner and held such sway over the party members and the people of the country. The Cuban economy was much more decentralized than the Soviet model and Castro now emphasized that workers must have material incentives to improve production in addition to the moral, idealistic and revolutionary incentives that had characterized the radical experiment. With sugar continuing to dominate its economy, Cuba became very dependent on Eastern Europe and the Soviet Union for necessary imports such as trucks, chemical fertilizers, pesticides, machinery, fuel (oil) and food. By the mid-1980s, strains in the relationship with the Soviet Union and Eastern Europe, coupled with debt problems, the lowest sugar prices since the Great Depression, corruption and growing economic inequality associated with the growth of peasant markets, led Castro to adopt another strategy—rectification—that, according to Pérez-Stable, "evoked the radical experiment of the 1960s." Thus, Castro was still trying to find the right mixture and balance of revolutionary principles and market-oriented pragmatism as the Cold War came to an end.

Yet, at the brink of the end of the Cold War Cuba had established one of the highest standards of living in the developing world and led all other Latin American countries in the quality of life that it provided for children. Its infant mortality rate was among the lowest in the world and it spent a higher percentage of its budget on education than any other country in Latin America. Rents were controlled and limited to 10 percent of income, rationed food prices were controlled and 80 percent of Cubans owned their own homes.[1] The pillars of the revolution—free healthcare, education and social security for all citizens—were rarely, if ever, found anywhere else in the developing world. At the same time, Castro, the revolutionary and pragmatist, was still firmly in control of the political decision-making on the island.

ECONOMIC CHANGE IN THE 1970s

Castro announced the failure of the 10-million-ton harvest on July 26, 1970, and took personal responsibility for it. It was clear that worker productivity had to be increased, government spending needed to be reduced and government revenues (especially in internationally accepted currencies) needed to be increased so that Cuba could pay for its imports and debts. The government implemented a series of changes in the country's economic strategy.

Low worker productivity, absenteeism and foot-dragging were to be corrected by providing more material incentives (wages and bonuses) based on increased production, the meeting of quotas and overtime work. The government increased the availability of consumer goods (televisions and refrigerators) so as to encourage workers to be more productive. Market-related reforms were introduced into the state-run enterprises. They were given greater authority to hire and fire workers, to use some of their profits to pay bonuses to outstanding workers, to purchase inputs from the private sector on the island and to hire workers on a piecemeal basis. Castro expanded the market-related reforms to include the agricultural and service sectors. The sugar industry became more mechanized with greater reliance placed on the use of combine harvesters to cut cane during the *zafra*. Castro became more tolerant of the private economic sector on the island. The growth of agricultural cooperatives was encouraged by providing them with greater access to new machinery while the growing of tobacco fell primarily to private farmers.[2] Farmers' markets were allowed so that cooperative and private farmers could sell their surpluses locally with prices based on supply and demand. The state also began to sell goods locally on a supply and demand basis. State-run stores with rationed goods at subsidized prices were still maintained to provide a social safety net for the poor. Self-employed individuals could provide certain services such as carpentry, plumbing, appliance and auto repair and housing construction.

In order to meet growing housing demands, Castro created the minibrigade system in the early 1970s. Approximately thirty-five workers who were released from their work commitments made up each minibrigade. These workers not only built prefabricated houses for individuals, but also community projects such as day care facilities, schools and medical clinics. The work centers or businesses that provided the workers for these minibrigades controlled 40 percent of the houses that were built and distributed them based on "social responsibility and merit." The level of family income determined the cost or rent to be paid for these units. Although the program had many problems, including the fact that these housing units were difficult to modify to meet the changing needs of families, and the national government controlled where these houses were built, it represented the first proactive state-financed approach to housing in all of Latin America.[3] By the end of the 1970s, more than 90 percent of the urban living units had running water and more than half had both running water and electricity.[4]

Castro expanded Cuba's trading ties by joining the Council for Mutual Economic Assistance (COMECON), an East European and Soviet Union trading block, in 1972. He also began to trade more with countries in the West. In fact, by 1974 the Western bloc accounted for 41 percent of the island's trade.[5] That year the island was benefiting from record high world sugar prices of 68 cents per pound.[6] Economic production increased dramatically. Between 1971 and 1975, the value of industrial output increased by 35 percent and the economy grew at an annual rate of 10 to 14 percent compared to 3.9 percent from 1966 to 1970.[7] Hard currency earnings (internationally accepted currency) from the sugar trade with the Western countries grew to almost $720 million in 1975.[8] Cuba began borrowing from Western banks during this period. It also benefited from the preferential trading policies of the Soviet Union. The Soviet Union continued to purchase Cuba's sugar at above world market prices and it provided oil at a price lower than the price provided by the Organization of Petroleum Exporting Countries. This helped to protect Cuba from the oil shocks of the early 1970s that caused severe economic problems for the United States and the West European countries. On the negative side, this relationship served as a disincentive for the diversification of the Cuban economy. Sugar remained the mainstay of the Cuban economy because of the lucrative price offered by the Soviet Union. The Soviet Union also provided Cuba with low-interest, long-term loans and a postponement on the payment of its immediate debts.

The tremendous growth of the economy led to growing expectations of a better life among most Cubans, but by 1977 the world market price of sugar had fallen dramatically to 8 cents a pound and the growth of the Cuban economy slowed considerably. With Cuba earning less from its sugar and its debts to Western countries mounting, Castro had to institute austerity measures that included the reduction of imports from Western countries. The favorable trading relationship with COMECON countries provided some protection for Cuba from the downturn in the price of sugar. The fact the Soviet Union and COMECON countries only purchased a few products from Cuba and continued to pay higher than world market prices forced the island to continue to depend on sugar as opposed to implementing policies designed to diversify its economy and to lessen its dependence on imports. With the slowdown in the economy, the number of houses built via the minibrigade program in the urban areas declined sharply. Dissatisfaction with the economy increased. At the same time, the government continued its commitment to the poor by providing its economic safety net of subsidized goods to all.

INSTITUTIONALIZATION

Castro attempted to institutionalize the revolution by drawing the jurisdiction lines of government more clearly. The PCC was to make political decisions, the state was to administer the policies and mass organizations, such as the Cuban Confederation of Labor (Confederacion de Trabajadores de Cuba; CTC), were to provide for popular participation. Cuba's first socialist constitution was adopted at the First PCC Congress in 1975 and approved through a referendum. It created the Popular Power system in which elected municipal assemblies elected members to the regional assemblies and the National Assembly. Municipal assemblies were given the authority to oversee policy in a variety of local services such as garbage, schools, street maintenance, clinics, grocery stores, theaters and small industries. According to scholar William Leogrande, the municipal assemblies have been quite successful in allowing for popular participation in these matters. The regional and national assemblies had limited power and for the most part ended up being a rubber stamp to major decisions already made within the Political Bureau of the PCC.

The PCC leadership organs (the Political Bureau, the Secretariat, and the Central Committee) that had not functioned in the 1960s began meeting regularly. The Central Committee, which was primarily made up of members from the military and the Ministry of the Interior in the 1960s, came to represent most sectors of Cuban society. The PCC experienced a dramatic increase in membership growing from 55,000 in 1969 to 211,642 in 1975, the year of Cuba's First PCC Congress. The Communist Youth became the primary avenue to party membership and by 1980 membership had reached 434,943.[9]

The CTC held periodic meetings. There was an increase in the number of local unions and there was a massive turnover in local union leadership throughout the 1970s through elections that used the secret ballot. In order to encourage more workers to join unions, they were represented on economic management boards and helped to develop local production targets and deal with health and safety issues. Increasing worker production was seen as the primary goal of unions. Material incentives (raises and bonuses) were tied to increased production and the quality of the goods produced. Unions were represented at all levels within the decision-making processes of the PCC and the Popular Power system.

The Federation of Cuban Women (Federacíon de Mujeres Cubanas; FMC) held congresses in 1974 and 1980. In 1975, Castro initiated a policy of affirmative action designed to increase the number of women in the PCC, the Popular Power system, the Communist Youth and the CTC. Increased membership at all levels of these institutions was realized by the late 1970s. Women's share of the labor force increased and the FMC was gradually successful in reducing the number of job categories that were reserved for men but still suffered from discrimination in achieving managerial positions.

CUBAN INTERNATIONALISM IN THE 1970s

Several factors contributed to the rise of Cuba as a force in international politics by the mid to late 1970s. Throughout the first half of the decade, Cuba's Revolutionary Armed Forces (Fuerzas Armadas Revolucionarias; FAR) underwent major changes. Many active military personnel were poorly trained, had little education and worked as agricultural laborers during the radical experiment of the 1960s. According to Richard Millett, a specialist on the Cuban military, in order to reduce these costs to the government the number of active military personnel of the FAR was reduced from 230,000 in 1970 to 117,000 in 1975. Training, equipment and weaponry for the military was upgraded significantly, largely due to the influence of the Soviet Union. The threat of a U.S.-led invasion of the island disappeared with the winding down of the Vietnam War and the arrival of détente between the Soviet Union and the United States and, as a result, the mission of the FAR became much more internationalist in orientation.

Cuba's isolation within Latin America also came to an end. Mexico never broke its relationship with Castro and eight other Latin American countries reestablished diplomatic ties between

1972 and 1975. The Organization of American States voted to end sanctions against Cuba in 1975. Castro was also busy establishing himself as a leader of the developing countries of the world. He traveled extensively throughout Africa in 1972 and 1973. His attendance at the Fourth Non-Aligned Summit in Algiers in 1973 marked Cuba's emergence as a leader among those countries. The Non-Aligned Movement (NAM) was made up of countries from Latin America, Africa and Asia that focused on issues of anticolonialism and economic development. The charismatic Castro, Cuba's economic success, its defiance of the United States and its anti-imperialist/anti-colonial message played well among the NAM countries.

In late 1975, Cuban troops intervened in the Angolan civil war that had broken out when the Portuguese empire in Africa began to crumble. Cuban troops supported the Popular Movement for the Liberation of Angola and were decisive in defeating the South African– and U.S.-backed groups. Cuban troops in support of Mengistu Haile Mariam's Ethiopian government also proved decisive in defeating a Somalian invasion of that country in 1977. Almost one out of every five Cuban soldiers served abroad in 1978 with most of them in Africa.[10] In July 1979, Castro's vision of a second revolution in Latin America finally came to pass with the Sandinista victory over the U.S.-supported Somoza dictatorship in Nicaragua. Cuban support of the Sandinistas during their struggle with Anastasio Somoza was very minimal when compared to its efforts in Africa and Castro advised the new Sandinista government to avoid conflicts with the United States and diversify its trading partners. He urged it to make economic policy changes very slowly so as to avoid the massive emigration of skilled and professional people that Cuba suffered in the first few years of its revolution. In September of that year, the Sixth Non-Aligned Summit was held in Havana, with Cuba exercising the primary leadership role in developing the anti-American tone of the Final Declaration. Prime Minister Michael Manley of Jamaica and Maurice Bishop of the New Jewel Movement in Grenada openly courted Castro. Cuba was at the height of its power in terms of global political influence in the late 1970s and the FAR was a major military force in the developing world.

Cuban internationalism of this period had another component that received little notice in the Western countries. This component sent thousands of Cuban doctors, teachers, construction workers, agronomists and other development project specialists (in irrigation, mining, fishing, cattle raising and sugar production) to Africa and other parts of the developing world. Most of this developmental aid was provided at either no cost to the host government or the host government simply covered the living expenses for the Cubans. By 1978, Cuba had more than 12,000 economic and technical aid specialists abroad and the number was greater than 14,000 in 1979.[11] These activities earned Cuba much prestige and respect among the developing countries of the world, especially those in Africa.

CUBA, THE UNITED STATES AND THE SOVIET UNION IN THE 1970s

In August 1970, a U.S. reconnaissance plane photographed the construction of a Soviet submarine base at the southern coastal city of Cienfuegos. President Richard Nixon argued that this violated the missile crisis agreement banning the introduction of offensive weapons systems in the Western Hemisphere. He successfully negotiated with the Soviet Union to stop the construction while the Cubans, once again, had little say in the issue. Just as in the missile crisis, Cuba remained a junior player in superpower politics. It was common in the United States to view the relationship between the Soviet Union and Cuba as one in which the Cubans merely followed the orders of the Soviet Union. This is not only simplistic, but also historically incorrect. Cuba and the Soviet Union shared a more complex and interdependent relationship. Cuban foreign policy was clearly at odds with the Soviet Union during most of the 1960s, with the Soviet Union not supporting Castro's efforts to wage revolutionary wars in Latin America. The relationship that eventually developed was one of mutual benefit in which each country received support in the pursuit of its own national goals. This became quite evident throughout the decade of the 1970s. Cuba received economic development assistance, technology, preferential trading partners and the means to upgrade its military. Cuban internationalism was a Cuban goal and the result of Cuban decisions. The intervention in Angola was a decision made by Castro. Development aid to Africa and other developing countries of the world was a Cuban decision. Because of its relationship with Cuba, the Soviet Union received a presence in the Caribbean, an area that has historically been within the sphere of influence of the United States. Perhaps more importantly, the Soviet Union also gained entry into many of the developing countries of the world because of Cuba's leadership role in NAM and the prestige and respect it had earned among those countries. Cuban foreign policy scholar H. Michael Erisman argues that Cuba established itself as a political broker between the Soviet Union and the developing countries of the world.

Castro, who did not trust Nixon and viewed him as the architect of the Bay of Pigs invasion, was quite pleased with his resignation in August 1974. This paved the way for a series of meetings between the United States and Cuba later that year and throughout much of 1975. These meetings reduced the tensions between the two countries temporarily. The Cubans preferred to focus primarily on specific issues that involved only the United States, such as payment for seized properties, immigration, the U.S. military base at Guantánamo Bay, the trade embargo, normalization of relations, surveillance flights and radio interference. The tendency of the United States was to link changes in the bilateral relationship with other issues such as Cuban ties to the Soviet Union and Cuban policies in Africa. President Gerald Ford ended all discussions with the island when the Cubans decided to send troops to Angola in late 1975.

President Jimmy Carter, who had a personal interest in Latin America, was elected in the wake of Watergate, Vietnam and Ford's pardon of Nixon. Although not happy with the presence of Cuban troops in Angola, Carter began making overtures to Castro. In April 1977, the United States and Cuba signed agreements concerning fishing rights and the maritime boundary in the Straights of Florida. Carter created a U.S. Interests Section in Havana in September and removed some of the restrictions on travel to the island by U.S. citizens. He began negotiating with Castro for the release of political prisoners. But Carter's moves to normalize relations with the island soured with the introduction of 20,000 Cuban troops in Ethiopia in January 1978. In an effort to maintain the lines of communication with the United States, Castro announced in September his willingness to dialogue with groups from the Cuban exile community and to release political prisoners. He also allowed thousands of Cuban exiles to return to the island as tourists to visit their families and relatives. These moves were designed to appeal to the human rights agenda of Carter and the one group that had the most influence over U.S.

policy toward Cuba. One of the consequences of these moves was a growing split within the Cuban American community in the United States. Some opposed the dialogue, while others supported it because they felt it would lead to the release of political prisoners. Many of those who participated in the dialogue with Castro received death threats from the militant Cuban American community, while others had to face boycotts of their businesses. Some even had their businesses bombed.[12]

By the end of 1979, it was impossible for Carter to make any more overtures to Cuba. The Sandinistas came to power in Nicaragua in July and some in the United States blamed Carter for the so-called communist victory in Central America. This, coupled with the growing rebel insurgency in El Salvador, made Carter appear to be weak and indecisive against communism. The taking of American hostages by the Iranians contributed to the appearance of a president weak in foreign affairs. This weakness was exploited by presidential candidate Ronald Reagan, who had staked out a conservative hard-line stance against not only communism, but also Carter's Panama Canal treaties and the Soviet invasion of Afghanistan. Politically, Carter was forced to take a harder line in foreign policy to meet the electoral challenge of Reagan.

THE 1980s, RECTIFICATION AND THE END OF THE COLD WAR

Castro knew that if Reagan were to be elected as president any meaningful accommodation with the United States would not be possible after January 1981. He allowed almost 125,000 Cubans to leave the country via the port city of Mariel in 1980. Among these émigrés were political prisoners, common criminals (less than 4 percent of the total), Cubans released from mental health facilities and Cuba's poor. Most were from the Havana area. This group differed significantly from the largely elite professionals and middle- and working-class immigrants who arrived in Miami during the first (1959–1962) and second (1965–1973) waves. Whereas the early immigrants were received with open arms, the Mariel group added to the growing racial tensions in Florida between Cubans and non-Cubans. The overwhelming media attention focused on the criminal element among the Mariel émigrés and Florida officials indicated that they could not provide the services, schools and jobs for needed for them.

Several factors help to explain this large exodus. The decline of the economy in the late 1970s following a period of tremendous economic growth had deflated the rising economic expectations among many Cubans and increased their sense of frustration. The appearance of thousands of comparatively wealthy Cuban American tourists returning to visit their relatives on the island added fire to the growing Cuban discontent. According to scholar Susan Eva Eckstein, the demand for unmet housing also probably contributed to the mass emigration from the port of Mariel. Castro's calculated decision to allow those who wanted to leave the freedom to do so was not only a last-minute appeal to the human rights agenda of the Carter administration and the international community, but also a clear opportunity to get rid of some of those who opposed him.

Ironically, the same year that tens of thousands of Cubans left the island from Mariel for economic reasons, the economy began to improve once again as the world price of sugar reached a yearly average of 28 cents per pound. Castro moved further to liberalize the Cuban economy by relaxing the regulations on foreign investment by allowing foreigners to have up to 49 percent ownership in local businesses.[13] The production of steel, medicines, electronics and chemicals increased. With the reduction in state-provided housing through the minibrigades, the private sector began meeting much of this demand. Housing construction in the early 1980s grew at a faster rate than any other sector and between 1981 and 1986 more than 60 percent of the housing units were privately constructed.[14] Production of agricultural goods increased largely due to the increase in price the state procurement agency paid to private farmers. In addition, both state and private workers realized increased profits from the farmers' markets.

The downside to the liberalization of the economy was that these lucrative markets encouraged farmers to sell their poorest crops to the state and their better-quality crops for even higher profits at the markets. This undermined the state's efforts to maintain the economic safety net for its poorest citizens. Public funds and resources used on state-run farms were often diverted illegally for private gain. Certain products were to be sold by the state and not supposed to be sold privately because they earned the government sorely needed foreign exchange or international currencies. These products, such as coffee, were routinely sold on the black market because of the profits to be earned. This practice cut into the state's ability to earn foreign exchange. Middlemen or vendors who bought from farmers and then sold goods at the markets appeared despite the fact they were illegal.

Cuban internationalism expanded in the early 1980s. Military equipment and training was provided to the Farabundo Marti National Liberation (Farabundo Marti para la Liberacion Nacional; FMLN) rebel forces in El Salvador, although the bulk of that was provided prior to the failed "final offensive" against the U.S.-supported government in 1981. Cuba provided military equipment, approximately 800 advisers and technical expertise to the Sandinistas of Nicaragua in their struggle against the Contra forces supported by the United States. It provided construction workers to twenty countries in Africa, Latin America, the Caribbean and Asia. Thousands of Cuban healthcare workers, doctors and teachers provided assistance to countries in the developing world. In 1980, Castro announced a change in its military policy. He created a militia made up of nonmilitary personnel (much like our National Guard) that numbered almost 1.5 million people. Castro later justified this in terms of responding to the aggressive nature of the Reagan administration but scholars, such as Millett, argue that it was done largely to mobilize and reinvigorate popular support for the revolution.

President Reagan, who viewed the world strictly through the East-West Cold War perspective, brought a desire to restore U.S. power in the world and implement a hard-line anticommunist foreign policy. He viewed Cuban internationalism as simply part of the Soviet Union's "evil empire." U.S. defense expenditures escalated sharply and aid to countries under the threat of communist or communist-inspired insurgencies increased dramatically. Reagan moved to topple the Sandinistas in Nicaragua by organizing and funding the opposition group known as the Contras. The U.S. invasion of Grenada in October 1983 toppled the left-wing government of Bernard Coard who had just toppled the government of Maurice Bishop. One of the stated reasons for the invasion was the use of Cuban military and construction workers on an airport that, according to the United States, was to be used for military purposes. Reagan did not mention publicly that the Cubans had won the construction contract against British, Canadian and French firms who all stated that the purpose of the airport was to increase tourism on the island. The United States increased military aid from $33.5 million in 1983 to $176.8 million the following year to prop up the government of El Salvador in its struggle against the FMLN.[15] Reagan moved quickly against Cuba by halting all air links with it and effectively banning travel to Cuba by prohibiting monetary expenditures on the island by U.S. citizens.

By 1984, the world market price of sugar had fallen to 5 cents a pound and the Cuban economy was once again in recession. The country suffered from increasing international debts, an increased cost of hard-currency imports due to the devaluation of the U.S. dollar and the need to increase foreign investments and government revenues. Even with the private construction of housing, there was still a shortage and the construction of clinics and day care facilities did not meet the nation's demand. Corruption had increased and was clearly associated with the growth of the peasant markets. Corruption took the form of stealing or diverting resources from state-run enterprises for private gain, the selling of the poorest crops to the state with the best crops being sold at the farmers' markets, the selling of illegal products on the black market and the illegal use of state goods in the construction of houses by private individuals. Castro viewed this as a breakdown in revolutionary community conscience. He argued that it was caused by excessive reliance on market forces and the desire for individual gain at the expense of community and society. By the mid-1980s, the CTC was also having accountability problems with workers of which nearly 50 percent either had been a child in 1959 or had been born after Castro came to power.[16] In addition, growing economic inequality between those who could divert their products to the lucrative peasant markets and those who could not do so challenged the egalitarian principles of the revolution.

Mikhail Gorbachev's revolutionary changes in the Soviet Union, which included economic and political liberalization under the labels of perestroika and glasnost, appeared at a time when Castro was initiating his own campaign for rectification. Castro and the aging revolutionary leadership reacted with hostility to the reforms of the Soviet Union and in Eastern Europe. Although publicly this hostility was explained in ideological terms, Castro also knew that these changes were a threat to the enormous economic subsidies and military support that Cuba received.

Castro initiated reforms in April prior to the PCC congress of December 1986 under the name of rectification—a return to the revolutionary idealism of the 1960s. He criticized the "profiteers" who were corrupt and had benefited at the expense of others and the state. Revolutionary idealism with its emphasis on community rather than private gain was emphasized once again. Imports were cut and wages were reduced except in the case of the poorest workers whose wages were actually increased. The peasant markets were eliminated although the state continued to sell some of its better products on a supply and demand basis in its *agromercados.* There was a return to the use of minibrigades to build houses, day care centers and schools, rather than depending on private contractors. This time, the state reimbursed the economic enterprises that supplied the workers for the minibrigades. Between 1984 and 1988, nearly half a million Cubans who were leaseholders on government-owned housing had their rents converted to payments for outright home ownership and another 330,000 were simply granted titles to their houses at no cost.[17] Volunteerism was reemphasized as the PCC adopted the slogan, "forty hours of voluntary work on community projects." The state continued to provide its social safety net for all through its subsidized and rationed food stores. Ironically, at the same time Castro was criticizing Cubans for acting like individualists and capitalists, he was encouraging Western investors and the promotion of joint investment ventures in electronics, mechanical engineering, petrochemicals, pharmaceuticals, textiles and tourism.[18] He also allowed private rentals and encouraged family-constructed housing units by making available low-interest building loans. Rectification was a mixture of revolutionary ideals and pragmatic, market-oriented policies.

Corruption among high-level government officials and military personnel was publicly exposed during the period of rectification. With Cuba's constant need for foreign exchange and hard currency, those in crucial government positions who interacted with Western companies and financial institutions were prone to corruption. They used their preferential access to key resources for their own personal benefit and many lived beyond the means of the typical Cuban citizen. Public trials combined with long-term prison sentences and some executions of top government officials were designed to deter future corruption. The most sensational and noteworthy trial was that of General Arnaldo Ochoa Sánchez, who was condemned to death for treason. The popular General Ochoa was a hero of Cuba's military triumphs in Angola and led missions to Ethiopia and Nicaragua. While in Angola, Ochoa had sold Cuban sugar, cement and other goods on the Angolan black market as well as supplementing his budget with shipments of diamonds and ivory to Western Europe, although much of this was done to improve the living conditions of Cuban troops in the field. At the time, these activities were overlooked in the name of Cuban internationalism.[19] With rectification policies in place, Cuban internationalism had also begun to contract. In particular, Cuba could no longer afford its large military presence in Africa. This policy caused resentment among many of the officers of the proud Cuban military. Returning military personnel faced a difficult economy when they returned home. General Ochoa was most vocal in his criticism of the cutbacks in the international mission of the FAR and the treatment of Cuban troops when they returned home from Africa to face economic austerity. Ochoa and other high-ranking military officials were also charged with drug trafficking. According to Millett, the evidence of drug trafficking against most of the defendants was strong, but that against Ochoa was extremely weak. Some scholars believe that the popular Ochoa had become a political threat either to Raúl Castro, head of the FAR, or Fidel Castro himself. Regardless, his execution provided a clear signal that loyalty to Castro was still perhaps the most important aspect of the revolutionary Cuban political system.

CUBA AT THE BRINK OF THE END OF THE COLD WAR

Despite the attempts to institutionalize the revolution through the PCC, the Popular Power assemblies and the CTC, the personal and charismatic rule of Castro was still the most important factor in providing legitimacy to the revolutionary government of Cuba. This was clearly evident in the fact that a special hand-picked PCC organ of his most loyal and trusted advisers, the Commandante en Jefe's Advisory Commission, existed. It was evident in the fact that rectification was Castro's idea. The PCC had little, if any, role in the decision. It merely approved Castro's policies. The fact that an extremely popular general could be executed also drove home the continuing importance of the personal significance of Castro to the revolution.

Although no one, including Castro, predicted the abrupt end of communism in Eastern Europe and the Soviet Union, it was clear that he knew that any change in the preferential relationship with these countries could threaten his own revolution. With the collapse of the Berlin Wall and of communism in Eastern Europe and the Soviet Union, Castro found Cuba truly independent for the first time in its history. Yet, that very independence threatened his revolution like no other event since 1959. Castro faced other problems at home. He faced a once-proud military that had seen its international mission collapse under budget cuts and soldiers returning home to an island that was in recession. He was saddled with an aging revolutionary leadership while the majority of the Cuban population had been born after 1959. In addition, in 1986 there was a massive turnover in the Central Committee of the PCC with almost 50 percent of the members being newly elected. The members were better educated than ever before and almost 40 percent of the PCC had been in the party less than five years.[20] His challenge was to "retire" some of the aging leadership and appeal to the younger generation. Leaders within the younger generation had to be sought out and brought into the ruling circles. Castro, the aging charismatic revolutionary and the ultimate Machiavellian political survivor, was forced to rise to the challenge of a post–Cold War world.

NOTES

1. Benjamin Keen and Keith Haynes, *A History of Latin America*, 6th ed. (Boston: Houghton Mifflin, 2000), 448.

2. Susan Eva Eckstein, *Back from the Future* (Princeton, N.J.: Princeton University Press, 1994), 45.

3. Ibid., 158–160.

4. Ibid., 160.

5. Ibid., 47, 51.

6. Ibid., 50.

7. Keen and Haynes, *History of Latin America*, 446; and Eckstein, *Back from the Future*, 51.

8. Eckstein, *Back from the Future*, 52.

9. Marifeli Pérez-Stable, *The Cuban Revolution* (Oxford: Oxford University Press, 1999), 146.

10. H. Michael Erisman, *Cuba's International Relations* (Boulder, Colo.: Westview, 1985), 73.

11. Ibid., 78–79.

12. María Cristina García, *Havana USA* (Berkeley: University of California Press, 1996), 47–52.

13. Eckstein, *Back from the Future*, 46.

14. Ibid., 161.

15. Peter H. Smith, *Talons of the Eagle* (New York: Oxford University Press, 2000), 215.

16. Pérez-Stable, *Cuban Revolution*, 128.

17. Eckstein, *Back from the Future*, 160.

18. Ibid., 68.

19. Andrés Oppenheimer, *Castro's Final Hour* (New York: Simon and Schuster, 1992), 141.

20. Pérez-Stable, *Cuban Revolution*, 144.

8

Post–Cold War Cuba and the Future

Since the late 1860s, Cuba has sought to become a truly independent country. In 1898, Spanish colonialism gave way to U.S. hegemony; in the 1960s, U.S. hegemony gave way to dependence on the Soviet Union. With the collapse of communist regimes in Eastern Europe and the Soviet Union in the early 1990s, Cuba found itself truly independent for the first time in its history. But, there is an old adage that says that one should be careful for what one wishes. Fidel Castro quickly realized that Cuba could not stand by itself and that new economic and political policies had to be implemented. These policies clearly reflect the recognition that Cuba can never be truly independent in the global political economy of today. These new policies also reflect a very pragmatic approach to Cuba's problems. Castro has been accused by many of being an ideologue who makes decisions solely on the basis of his own version of Marxist-Leninist ideology. Historically speaking, this has never been the case and nowhere is this pragmatism more evident than in the policy reforms of the post–Cold War era.

It is perhaps this pragmatism that will allow Cuba to survive in the global economy of the twenty-first century.

THE SPECIAL PERIOD AND ECONOMIC REFORM

With the fall of communism in Eastern Europe and the subsequent fall of the Soviet Union during the period 1989–1991, Soviet petroleum exports to Cuba dropped by 25 percent in 1990 and by 1992 oil shipments had declined from a high of 13 million tons in 1989 to 1.8 million tons. Food shipments dropped by more than 50 percent in 1991 and the Cuban economy contracted by as much as 50 percent between 1989 and 1992.[1] During this so-called Special Period, Castro placed Cubans on a wartime economy. Austerity measures were put in place. Wages became stagnant and purchasing power plummeted. Fuel shortages, planned and unplanned electrical blackouts, factory shutdowns and transportation problems were common. Food shortages were becoming a problem and rationing reappeared, although it should be noted that rationing more than likely prevented the massive malnutrition and hunger that is common in many of the developing countries. Living standards that had improved tremendously the previous two decades were reversed. Expectations of higher living standards were shattered and there was a clear and growing disillusionment with Castro. In 1992 and 1993, more than 7,000 *balseros* (the name given to those who braved the Straits of Florida in makeshift boats or rafts) made it to the United States from Cuba. According to interviews, the vast majority of the *balseros* were escaping the economic hardships of the Special Period.[2]

In order to survive, Cuba was forced to make major economic policy changes. It needed new sources for its imports, new markets for its exports and access to technology, capital (funds for investment) and international currencies (foreign exchange). It needed to diversify its economy and increase food production for local consumption. At the same time, Castro and the Cuban people were convinced that these policy reforms had to be made without threatening the revolutionary social safety net of free education, healthcare and social security benefits guaranteed to all.

One of the major problems for the island during the Special Period was that it lacked the foreign exchange to pay for its imports and debts. In perhaps the most significant reform, the U.S.

dollar was legalized in August 1993. Before this, it was a crime for Cubans to hold U.S. dollars even though more than $400 million in U.S. currency per year was brought into the country via Cuban exiles living in the United States. These dollars fed the black market and served as an underground currency. Given that the government needed U.S. dollars to pay its debts and to purchase imports, the decision to legalize the dollar allowed the government to capture this needed foreign exchange. It could pay its debts and purchase products on the world market. In addition, one of the outcomes of this reform was that Cuba had two economies—one based on the U.S. dollar and the other on the Cuban peso with the dollar being the preferred unit of exchange.

Sugar was the largest source of foreign exchange for the government prior to the Special Period. Cuba was dependent on the discounted fuel (oil) and the higher-than-world market prices that it received from the Soviet Union and the East European countries. With the arrival of the Special Period, this subsidy came to an end. Due to bad weather and the lack of fuel, spare parts for machinery and fertilizer, sugar production in 1993 was lower than anytime since 1970. The dramatic decline in oil imports also hurt the nickel industry, which was also a major earner of foreign exchange. Thus, by 1994 tourism generated more income (foreign exchange) for Cuba than sugar. The decision was made to encourage the growth of tourism on the island. Foreign investment was needed to diversify the economy and promote the growth of the tourist industry.

In September 1995, the Cuban government dramatically changed the law concerning foreign investments on the island. Both joint ventures (a business owned in part by Cuba and in part by foreign investors) and complete foreign ownership of companies were legalized. Most investment capital comes from Spain, Venezuela, Canada, Italy, Mexico, Holland and the United Kingdom, although more than fifty other countries have investments on the island. Companies such as Sherritt (Canada), ING Bank (Netherlands), Western Mining (Australia), Grupo Domos (Mexico), Unilever (UK/Netherlands), Labatt (Canada) and Pernod Ricard (France) have invested in Cuba. Joint ventures are present in many areas of the economy today, such as telephones, hotels, mining, electricity, finance, natural gas, real estate and soft drinks. The French company Elf Aquitaine entered into a joint agreement with Cubapetroleo, Cuba's state-run energy firm, to pack liquid propane and a butane gas mix in cylinders and distribute them to households in eastern Cuba.

In order to attract more investment from abroad, the government studied free trade zones (FTZs) in Latin American and the Caribbean. Three FTZs were created in Havana and Mariel. Goods brought into these FTZs from within Cuba or from abroad are not subject to taxes. Manufacturers receive up to a twelve-year tax holiday to invest and enjoy the benefits of a highly educated workforce and a controlled labor environment. There are more than 290 companies conducting business in the FTZs. Companies in the FTZs are also able to sell part of their products in the domestic market. Economic changes involving foreign investment on the island also affected agriculture. Reforms made it easier to invest in the production of citrus, tobacco, vegetables and rice. By the middle of 1994, Spain was investing in the production of tobacco and Israel in the production of citrus. It is estimated that the joint Cuban-Israeli enterprise in Jaguey Grande (east of Havana) produces 36 percent of the island's total citrus production today.[3]

The tourist industry has also attracted much foreign investment. Hotel chains from Canada (Delta, Commonwealth and Hospitality LTD), Spain (Iberostar SA, Sol-Melia, RUI Hotels SA and Raytur) and Jamaica (Super-Club) have made major investments. Hundreds of thousands of Canadian and European tourists come to Cuba each year to enjoy the five-star hotels and some of the finest beaches in the Caribbean. Cuba also attracts tens of thousands of illegal tourists from the United States each year. Funds from the tourist industry are being used to renovate World Heritage Sites in Habana Vieja (Old Havana) and the city of Trinidad.

The traditional agricultural model, which had been in place since the early 1970s, emphasized large, mechanized state-run farms and was almost totally dependent on imports of trucks, machinery, chemical fertilizers, pesticides, specialized feed and fuel (oil). Even the cutting of sugar cane became dependent on the use of combine harvesters. This traditional model played a role in the large number of Cubans who left agricultural work and moved to the urban areas during the 1970s and 1980s. During this same period, peasants, who traditionally supplied food for local consumption and were the primary beneficiaries of the revolutionary education reforms, also began moving from the rural areas to the cities. As a result, production of food for local consumption de-

clined and was replaced by imports during this period. Cuba relied almost entirely on the Council of Mutual Economic Assistance
countries (Eastern Europe and the Soviet Union) for these crucial
imports. Its agricultural sector was thrown into a crisis when these
imports were dramatically cut from 1989 to 1992.

In response to the agricultural crisis, reforms during the Special
Period included the setting aside of land on all state farms and
cooperatives for the production of food for local consumption.
State farms and cooperatives began developing livestock for consumption by their workers and members. By 1993, individual
farmers were also beginning to grow food locally to provide for
themselves and their workers. According to agriculture development specialist Laura Enriquez, the policy of providing food for
workers on state farms, cooperatives and individual farms helped
to ensure the labor supply in the agricultural sector. State farm
managers were allowed to "loan" some of their lands to *parceleros*,
who could use the land to grow crops for self-consumption. In
1993, the Cuban government started to move away from its traditional emphasis on large state-run farms. State farms have traditionally suffered from low productivity by workers, but with
the problems created by the Special Period and the disastrous
sugar crop in 1993, the decision was made to allow state farms to
be transformed into member-operated cooperatives in which the
members have usufruct rights (they do not own the land, they
only own the products produced from the land) and operate on
a profit-sharing basis. By 1994, all of the state-run sugar farms had
been transformed into member-operated cooperatives and state-
run farms in other agricultural areas were also being transformed.[4]
These reforms, which decentralized agricultural production and
moved to a more market basis for operation, led to a 17.3 percent
growth in agricultural production by 1996.[5]

Throughout the Special Period, the shortage of food crops created a very active black market. These goods were expensive and
only Cubans who had access to dollars could purchase them. In
October 1994, the government legalized, once again, the farmers'
markets, where surplus crops could be sold for profit. As a result,
black market sales declined, the availability of food at the markets
increased and food prices dropped. The government also overlooked the problem of health hazards and allowed the breeding
of pigs in Havana Province. The purpose of this was to provide

families with more pork (the favorite meat of Cubans and the source of lard) and to undermine the sale of it on the black market.

The Cuban government also began to allow self-employment in many different trades such as chauffeurs, hair stylists, shoemakers, photographers, carpenters and auto and bicycle repair. Those individuals who are self-employed are taxed by the state. Private home restaurants (*paladares*), legalized in 1993, are now common throughout the island and cater to both tourists and locals. These private restaurants must be licensed by the state and they advertise primarily through word of mouth, especially among tourist groups. They are taxed by the state and if they conduct business in U.S. dollars they must pay the tax in dollars.

The government made major cuts in spending in state-run enterprises, government investments and the military. State-run enterprises were also given autonomy and required to operate on their own accounts. In other words, state-run enterprises were now being asked to function on a for-profit basis. Many state-run enterprises were also given the ability to import necessary equipment and items without state permission. In order to improve its fiscal situation, the government levied a tax on some consumer goods. The government, to its credit, did not cutback spending on healthcare, education and social security. This continues to set Cuba apart from the remainder of the developing world and even some wealthy countries.

By 1996, it was clear that the economy was growing once again and that Cuba had survived the worst of the Special Period. Yet, the reforms were having some unanticipated outcomes. In particular, the dual existence of the dollar and peso economies was beginning to bring about a visible gap between the rich or the privileged and the poor. The privileged work in the tourist and service industries that have access to dollars. The poor are those trapped in the peso economy of the ration card and state-run stores. Even though this provides a basic standard of living due to the guaranteed social safety net, the peso economy is not able to provide the "extras" that access to dollars can provide. In particular, this places a difficult burden on white-collar professionals who work for the state, such as doctors, nurses, teachers, engineers, government administrators and others. Their monthly peso income allows them a basic standard of living but does not allow them to "get ahead." Many professionals have second jobs in the tourist sector as taxi drivers, where they can earn much more in

U.S. dollars. In a discussion with one professional on the island, he indicated that he was having difficulty convincing his son that he should attend college and go on to medical school. His son argued that he could make more money driving a taxi for tourists and he questioned the value of further education.[6] This presents a major dilemma for a country that invests so much in education. What is most evident is that resentment among those in the peso economy is growing and the egalitarian ideal of the revolution is clearly being threatened by the dual dollar and peso economies.

THE SPECIAL PERIOD AND MILITARY AND POLITICAL REFORMS

The end of the Cold War and the Special Period dramatically affected the Cuban Revolutionary Armed Forces (Fuerzas Armadas Revolucionarias; FAR). All military assistance, weapons and supplies deliveries came to an end. Spare parts for military vehicles, ships and aircraft became difficult to find. Fuel shortages forced reductions in vehicle and aircraft operations. Training exercises were reduced. The budget for the FAR was cut considerably. The FAR's highly successful internationalist mission came to an end in 1992 with the last personnel leaving Africa the previous year. Morale, which was already low due to the purges of the western army in the mid-1980s and the General Arnaldo Ochoa Sánchez affair, plummeted even further. The last Russian troops left the island in 1993.

One of the major reforms is that the mission of the FAR has changed. In 1991, Castro announced that the FAR must help with the economy. This was not unprecedented in the revolutionary era as it had exercised some administration of economic activities and provided labor for the sugar harvests during the 1960s. It was also already involved in the production of food by 1990 in order to meet its own consumptive needs during the Special Period. Soldiers returning from abroad were put to work on farms run by the state, while officers with technical expertise were put to work to find alternatives to the island's dependence on imported fertilizers. The FAR was given the authority to create economic enterprises to begin to meet some of its own budgetary needs. Gaviota is a joint venture with foreign investment that plays a major role in the growing tourist industry of Cuba. It also provides hard currency for the FAR and employment for retired service personnel. Since then, several subsidiaries have been created, such as Texnotec, which imports information technology and electronic equipment, and Tucrimex, which focuses on the movement of cargo. Another is the Ejercito Juvenil del Trabajo (EJT). The EJT has two enterprises in Jaguey Grande and the Isle of Youth that produce 58 percent of the island's citrus.[7] Another major reform is that the size of the military has been reduced considerably. The International Institute for Strategic Studies in London estimates that the Cuban military consisted of 105,000 troops in 1995. This represented a reduction of 100,000 troops since the mid-1980s. Mandatory military service for Cubans was reduced from three to two years. According to Richard Millett, a specialist on civil-military relations in Latin America, the current military has expressed doubts concerning the ability of the Cuban air force and tanks to defend the island from an invasion. Instead, it now focuses on guerrilla warfare and the "retreat into Cuba's mountains and rural areas" to defeat an attack on the island.

The Special Period also brought about an increase in crime, corruption and theft in the urban and rural areas. Dissident groups on the island increased and became more vocal in challenging authorities. The government responded with both repression and reform. In 1991, the Communist Party of Cuba (Partido Comunista de Cuba; PCC) opened its ranks to those who believe in God and the following year the country was declared to be secular rather than atheist. The political system was reformed in 1993 by allowing the election of members to all levels of the Popular Power assemblies rather than just the municipal level. Noncommunist candidates were allowed to run for office and some have been elected. In 1995, Concilio Cubano, an umbrella organization for human rights groups in Cuba, called for a national meeting. The group was denied recognition by the government and in early 1996 more than 200 human rights leaders were harassed, arrested and interrogated. One should note, however, that the number of political prisoners has declined steadily since 1991 and more than 300 were released after Pope John Paul II's historic visit in 1998. Amnesty International's 2002 Human Rights Report indicated a significant decrease in the number of political prisoners being held by Castro. At the same time, the report criticized Castro for his continued harassment of dissidents, the denial of civil rights to his people and the fact that he still holds political prisoners.

In 1991, the Political Bureau of the PCC was expanded in size but it excluded two important revolutionary figures: Vilma Espin, the president of the Federation of Cuban Women (Federacíon de Mujeres Cubanas), and Minister of Culture Armando Hart. In 1992, Manuel Pineiro, a former guerrilla commander, lost his position as the head of the Central Committee's espionage service. Ramiro Valdes, a former guerrilla captain nicknamed Red Beard, was removed as head of the powerful Ministry of the Interior in 1994. By 1995, ten of the fourteen provincial PCC secretaries were replaced with younger members. In the same year, seven younger individuals became heads of various economic ministries within the Council of State. In 1997, Carlos Rafael Rodriguez, a leader of the Popular Socialist Party (Partido Socialista Popular) in the 1950s, was removed from the Political Bureau of the PCC and in the same year Hart was relieved of his duties as minister of culture. It was clear that Castro was beginning to bring the next generation of loyal leaders into the ruling circles of Cuba.

RELATIONS WITH THE UNITED STATES IN THE POST–COLD WAR ERA

One may have expected the policy of the United States toward Cuba to change in the early 1990s with the collapse of communism in Eastern Europe, the establishment of a closer relationship between the United States and the Mikhail Gorbachev–led Russia and a continuation of the U.S. relationship with China despite the events of Tienamen Square. In addition, three of the four stated conditions necessary for U.S. normalization of relations had been met by 1992. Castro was no longer supporting revolutionaries in Latin America, Cuban military ties to the Soviet Union were, in effect, eliminated and all Cuban troops had been removed from Africa. The only condition left was an improvement in the protection of human rights on the island and a 1989 State Department report indicated improvement in this area. President George H. W. Bush even vetoed a bill in 1990 that would have made it difficult for subsidiaries of U.S. companies in other countries to trade with Cuba. In this case, the lobbying efforts of IBM, Exxon, ITT and others that traded with Cuba via third countries were successful.[8] It looked like President Bush was moving to change U.S. policy toward the island.

But the presidential election of 1992 and the power of the anti-Castro Cuban American National Foundation (CANF) brought an abrupt end to any thaw in U.S. policy. President Bush added the condition that Cuba must hold free and fair elections before the United States would consider normalizing relations. A similar version of the 1990 bill, the Cuban Democracy Act, also known as the Torricelli Act, was reintroduced in 1992. With Democratic presidential candidate Bill Clinton catering to CANF, President Bush decided to support the passage of the bill and signed it in Miami just before the election. The Torricelli Act prevents subsidiaries of U.S. companies in other countries from trading with Cuba even if those countries allow trade with the island. It also prevents ships that dock in Cuba from coming to the United States for six months and allows the president to stop U.S. foreign aid to any country that conducts business with Cuba. Finally, it allows the president to give assistance to Cuban dissidents. Even though Canada and U.S. allies in Europe opposed the Torricelli Act and resented what they considered to be U.S. intervention into their own trade policies, President Bush and the incoming President Clinton continued to take a hard line against Cuba.

Due to the crisis created with the arrival of the *balseros* during the Special Period, President Clinton worked with Cuban officials to promote safe, legal and orderly immigration to the United States. The United States agreed to allow a minimum of 20,000 legal Cuban immigrants per year. Clinton then moved to promote more people-to-people contacts between the United States and Cuba by allowing private organizations to develop relationships with Cuban organizations. The Cuban Liberty and Democratic Solidarity Act, also known as the Helms-Burton Act, made its way through Congress in 1996. Fearing an adverse reaction from U.S. allies in Europe and Canada, Clinton threatened a veto, but on February 24 of that year Cuban planes shot down two U.S. civilian aircraft belonging to the anti-Castro Miami-based group Brothers to the Rescue in international waters. In reaction to this event, the U.S. Congress passed and President Clinton signed the Helms-Burton Act in March. This act allows American citizens to sue foreign corporations whose trade or investments profit from any properties that were expropriated by the Castro government after 1959. It allows the U.S. government to penalize foreign companies that conduct business in Cuba. Finally, the act added another condition for the normalization of relations with Cuba: that no government with Castro or his brother Raúl would be acceptable to the United States. The assumption is that it would be unacceptable to the United States if either Castro were elected president through free and fair elections.

Yet, throughout the 1990s some dissenting voices concerning U.S. policy toward Cuba were raised. The same year the Torricelli Act was passed, the UN General Assembly voted overwhelmingly to condemn the U.S. embargo and each year since then it has done the same. At a summit meeting in 1993, Latin American, Spanish and Portuguese leaders unanimously called for an end to the embargo. The Organization of American States condemned the Helms-Burton Act and the Inter-American Juridical Committee ruled that it violates international law on at least eight counts. Most international law specialists argued that it violates several international treaties and Canada and the European countries argued that the United States has no right to extend its laws to their countries. They threatened to take the dispute before the World Trade Organization, but the Clinton administration worked out an agreement with them that he would not enforce the part of the Helms-Burton Act that allows U.S. citizens to sue foreign corporations that have benefited from expropriated properties in Cuba if they would support the demand for political reform on the island.

By the mid to late 1990s, it was clear to many agriculture and tourist businesses in the United States that they were missing out on the economic opening of Cuba under its reformed investment and trade policies. The United States–Cuba Trade Economic Council testified to Congress in 1998 in support of ending the U.S. embargo. Other large multinational corporations such as Archer Daniels Midland, Time Warner, Carghill and Caterpillar are on record in support of an end to the embargo. Pope John Paul II, who visited the island that same year, urged the United States to end its embargo. In reaction to the pope's visit, the Clinton administration allowed an increase in direct flights to the island, gave authority for direct food and medicine sales to Cuba and established direct mail service. In 2000, the United States passed a law that allowed the sale of agricultural commodities and medicine to Cuba on a cash basis only. Cuba agreed to purchase $73 million in grain, but this has been delayed due to President George W. Bush's refusal to grant visas to Cuban officials who have to come to the United States to finalize the deal.

Perhaps the primary obstacle to a change in U.S. policy is the importance of the state of Florida in the presidential election. This was clear to all in Bush's narrow electoral victory over Al Gore in 2000. This, coupled with the fact that his brother Jeb is the Florida governor and that Cuban Americans in Florida voted overwhelmingly in favor of George Bush in the 2000 election and Jeb Bush in the 2002 election, it seems that U.S. policy toward Cuba will not change significantly under President Bush. In May 2002, former president Jimmy Carter made a historic visit to the island. Carter is the only U.S. president to visit Cuba since 1959. He spoke live, uncensored and in Spanish on Cuban television. Carter urged the island to make the transition to democracy while calling for the United States to end the embargo. That same month, President Bush reiterated his hard-line stance against Cuba before a passionate, Miami audience of anti-Castro Cuban Americans.

THE FUTURE OF CUBA

Cuba at the turn of the twenty-first century is undergoing a transition similar to what occurred at the turn of the twentieth century. At that time, Cuban leadership, the United States and world economic forces interacted in such a way to usher in a period of U.S. hegemony. The United States flexed its regional power while world economic forces limited the options available to the newly "independent" country of Cuba. The Cuban economy was devastated after years of warfare. The nationalist Cuban leadership that had been decimated during the wars of independence was weak and unable to counter the power of the United States and the market forces of the world economy. Cuba became politically, economically and, to a lesser extent, culturally dominated by its neighbor to the north. Today, Castro, the United States and world economic forces are interacting in such a way to integrate Cuba further into the global market place. Yet, the biggest difference between the transition into the twentieth century and the transition into the twenty-first century is that, at least in the near future, Cuban leadership—Castro—will have more influence over the process of change than the United States and the world economy. Most people understand that U.S. policy toward the island is largely a function of its domestic politics and is not likely to change dramatically in the next few years. The self-imposed U.S. embargo to some extent serves to limit the American ability to influence the future direction of Cuba. The embargo is a blunt, singular tool of U.S. power. There are no U.S. government, busi-

ness, social and cultural organizations on the island that historically have provided the United States not only with more ways
to exercise its power, but also the ability to exercise its power in
more subtle, and perhaps longer lasting, ways. Thus, the United
States is unable to use perhaps its most important weapon: its soft
power. This means that Castro will have a much greater say over
the future of the island than did his nationalist counterparts at the
turn of the twentieth century.

At the same time, Castro was forced to respond to changes in
the world political economy during the Special Period. He has
adopted gradual, pragmatic, market-oriented policy changes to
meet Cuba's needs for energy, key imports, markets for its own
exports, technology, capital and foreign exchange. The questions
remain as to how far the Cuban economy will adopt market-
oriented reforms and how quickly this inevitable integration into
the world economy will take place. The answers will depend
largely on the degree to which these changes affect the growing
gap between the rich and the poor and the ability of the country
to maintain its revolutionary social safety net of free healthcare,
education and social security. Castro has shown that he is like
Cuban leaders of the past: he does not like to share power. Yet,
he is different from all leaders of the past because he has created
and is committed to maintaining a more economically egalitarian
Cuba.

The real threat to Castro's political power comes from within
the country. In one way, one could argue that he may fall victim
to his own successes. By achieving one of the most literate and
highly educated citizenry in the world and by achieving a revolutionary social safety net found nowhere else in the developing
world, he has created a set of high expectations and desires among
his people. The desire for greater political freedoms is a natural
outgrowth of this success. Repression of those who desire political
reform may be a short-term solution, but in the long term, history
has proven it never to be a successful strategy. At the same time,
the failure to continue to meet those high expectations can lead to
frustration and dissatisfaction within a population. This is clearly
evident today among those Cubans who do not have access to the
dollar economy and who are witnessing the growing gap between
the privileged and the poor. Finally, dissatisfaction among Cubans
is more acute because they continue to compare their living standards to those in the United States and are constantly reminded

from relatives and friends living there that they are poorer than Americans.

Castro is a bundle of contradictions. He is an idealist and a realist. He can be an ideologue and a pragmatist. He is capable of 180-degree shifts in policies. He can be cooperative and obstinate. He can be gentle and ruthless. He generates both love and hatred. He has had tremendous successes and tremendous failures. In the end, he is a political survivor that loves to play the game of politics and power. He is a revolutionary that challenged U.S. dominance as no Cuban leader has ever done and has maintained his revolutionary commitments to free education, cradle-to-grave healthcare and social security to all. He is a classic Latin American *caudillo* in that he does not like to share political power.

As the revolutionary generation in Cuba grows older with Castro, the post-Castro era will be on us within the next decade or two. There are several possible post-Castro scenarios that scholars have put forward. The official replacement is Raúl, head of the FAR and Castro's brother. The problem with Raúl is that he is only four years younger than his brother and is neither popular nor respected among most Cubans. Lacking his brother's charisma and support, he more than likely would have to resort to increased repression. Some have suggested that the exile community in the United States will step in and govern the country. These groups clearly have the economic capital that Cuba sorely needs but lack legitimacy among Cubans in general and with the FAR. They have also shown tendencies within the United States to be just as corrupt and intolerant as past Cuban leaders and governments.

Others suggest that the FAR will step in and rule the country, at least for a brief period, should Castro die suddenly and there is a struggle for power. The FAR suffers from morale problems and many of its officers are disillusioned with the current Cuban leadership that has cut its budget and internationalist mission. At the same time, the military is the best-organized and best-educated group in the country. Given its growing role in the economy of the island, it stands to lose much should the current government quickly come to an end and a power vacuum appear. Some have suggested that the FAR could stage a *golpe* and actually seize power from Castro. Others suggest that this is probably unlikely. The FAR has no history of this type of activity and its mission and culture blends both political and military functions much like that of China and Vietnam. It has never been an autonomous actor within the decision-making processes in Cuba. Its leaders are loyal to the Castro brothers and a large percentage of the Central Committee of the PCC consists of military officers. These factors clearly mitigate the likelihood of a *golpe* against Castro.

Other scholars argue that Cuba will follow the same path as the East European countries or the former Soviet Union. A post-Castro leadership will eventually arise that is less committed to real democracy and more committed to restructuring the economy and placing itself in position to take advantage of massive privatization that will take place under the auspices of the World Bank, the International Monetary Fund, the United States and other wealthy countries of the world. Under such neoliberal economic restructuring, it is clear that the social safety net, Castro's real revolutionary success, will disappear. Those who benefited the most from the revolution will see their standard of living decline while foreign companies and a few at the top of Cuban society will benefit enormously. Trying to predict the future of a country is virtually impossible. It is difficult to say what a post-Castro Cuba will look like, but the history of the island has shown that the future will be written by Cuban leaders who will have to struggle with the forces of the world economy and the power of the United States. These are the constants in the history of the island and they will be the constants in its future.

NOTES

1. Laura Enriquez, "Cuba's New Agricultural Revolution: The Transformation of Food Crop Production in Contemporary Cuba," *Food First, Development Report* no. 14 (May 2000): 4.

2. *Christian Science Monitor*, 6 February 1991; *Boston Globe*, 2 January 1994, 9.

3. Maria Antonia Fernandez Mayo and James E. Ross, "Cuba: Foreign Agribusiness Financing and Investment," International Working Paper IW98–7, EDIS, University of Florida, 1998, 13.

4. Enriquez, "Cuba's New Agricultural Revolution," 4.

5. Benjamin Keen and Keith Haynes, *A History of Latin America*, 6th ed. (Boston: Houghton Mifflin, 2000), 453.

6. Interview by the author, Havana, May 2001.

7. Mayo and Ross, "Cuba," 13.

8. Economic Intelligence Unit, *Cuba Country Report*, no. 3 (1990): 16.

Notable People in the History of Cuba

Reinaldo Arenas (1943–1990). A poet, novelist and writer of international reputation who was convicted in 1973 for ideological deviation and publishing abroad without official consent. He came to the United States in 1980 during the Mariel exodus. He is perhaps best known for his book *Before Night Falls*.

Francisco de Arrango y Parreno (1765–1839). A Creole planter and Cuban nationalist who promoted the sugar industry in the late 1700s and early 1800s. He successfully lobbied Charles III of Spain to allow free and unlimited importation of slaves to Cuba.

Fulgencio Batista y Zaldivar (1901–1973). A mulatto army sergeant who came to dominate Cuban politics from 1933 to 1959. He led the sergeants' revolt that toppled Gerardo Machado in 1933 and then a *golpe* in 1952 to seize the presidency. His corrupt and repressive government was toppled by Fidel Castro in 1959. He died in exile in Spain.

Fidel Castro Ruz (1926–). The charismatic, bearded leader of the revolution that toppled the Batista dictatorship, he has ruled the country since 1959. His father owned a sugar plantation in Oriente. Castro studied law at the University of Havana and led the attack on the Moncada Barracks in Santiago in 1953.

Raúl Castro Ruz (1930–). He is the brother of Fidel Castro and a leader of the 26th of July Movement. He is currently the minister of defense and chief of the armed forces of Cuba.

Carlos Manuel de Céspedes (1819–1874). He was a Creole planter from Bayamo who declared Cuban independence and started the Ten Years' War in 1868. Some consider him to be the father of modern Cuba.

Eduardo Chibas (1907–1951). He was a charismatic student leader and leader of the Ortodoxo Party. He greatly influenced Fidel Castro and was a candidate for the presidency in 1952. He committed suicide during a radio broadcast in 1951.

Camilo Cienfuegos (–1959). He was a very popular commander of the 26th of July Movement who was killed in a plane crash in 1959.

Bishop Diaz de Espada (1756–1832). He was one of the founders of the Economic Society in the early 1800s. He was responsible for liberalizing the curriculum at the Real Colegio Seminario de San Carlos in Havana that became the breeding ground for Cuban nationalists in the 1800s.

Jose Antonio Echeverria (–1957). He was a charismatic student leader who was president of the Federation of University Students and organized the Revolutionary Directorate that waged an urban terrorist war against Fulgencio Batista. He was killed in 1957 leading an attack on Batista. He was perhaps the only person capable of challenging Fidel Castro as the leader of the revolutionary groups.

Vilma Espin (1931–). She was an original member of the 26th of July Movement and the assistant to Raúl Castro in the Sierra

Maestra. She later married Raúl. She is the president of the Cuban Federation of Women.

Evaristo Estenoz (–1912). He was a former slave and veteran of the Cuban wars for independence. He became the leader of the Independent Party of Color that led an African uprising in 1912 that was crushed by Cuban and U.S. troops.

Tomás Estrada Palma (1835–1908). He was the first president of the Republic of Cuba from 1902 until 1906, when the second U.S. occupation of the island began.

Mario García Menocal (1886–1941). He fought in the Cuban wars for independence and was president of the Republic of Cuba from 1913 to 1921.

Máximo Gómez (1836–1905). He was a Dominican that led the rebel military forces in the Ten Years' War against Spain.

Ramón Grau San Martín (1887–1969). He was the dean of the medical school at the University of Havana, leader of the Autentico Party and president of the Republic of Cuba from 1933 to 1934 and 1945 to 1949. When Grau was president in 1933, he came to represent the goals and dreams of the Generation of 1930.

Ernesto "Che" Guevara (1928–1967). From Argentina, he was a commandant of the 26th of July Movement and a confidant of Fidel Castro. He was an intellectual and wrote extensively on guerrilla warfare. He died in an ill-fated attempt to stage a revolution in Bolivia in 1967.

Antonio Maceo (1845–1896). He is known as the "Bronze Titan," and was perhaps the most effective rebel general during the wars for independence from Spain.

Gerardo Machado (1871–1939). He was president of the Republic of Cuba from 1925 to 1933. His corrupt and repressive regime set the groundwork for the sergeants' revolt of 1933 led by Fulgencio Batista.

José Martí (1853–1895).   He was an intellectual, poet, statesman and revolutionary. He is considered to be the father of Cuban independence.

Julio Antonio Mella (1905–1929).   A charismatic student leader, he was secretary of the Federation of University Students and the first student leader of the Generation of 1930 to become a national figure. He was exiled in 1927 and murdered in Mexico two years later on orders from Cuban president Gerardo Machado.

José Miguel Gómez (1858–1921).   He was leader of the Liberal Party and second president of the Republic of Cuba from 1909 to 1913.

Arnaldo Ochoa Sánchez (1930–1989).   He joined the 26th of July Movement and fought with Camilo Cienfuegos during the revolution. His distinguished military career included command of Cuban troops in Angola. He was accused of drug trafficking and treason in 1989 and was executed. Some argue that he had become so popular that he was a political threat to either Fidel or Raúl Castro.

Carlos Prio Socarras (1903–1977).   He represented the Autentico Party and was the president of the Republic of Cuba from 1949 to 1952.

Jose Antonio Saco (1797–1879).   He was a leading intellectual and nationalist in the 1800s. He supported Cuban self-rule and an end to slavery.

Celia Sánchez (–1980).   She served with Castro in the Sierra Maestra. She was Castro's personal secretary and confidant until her death from cancer in 1980.

Haydee Santamaria (–1980).   She and her brother, Abel, were with Castro in the attack on Moncada. She ran the 26th of July Movement's fund-raising activities in Miami, served as a member of the Central Committee of the Communist Party of Cuba and headed the revolutionary government's cultural center. She committed suicide in 1980.

Tomás Terry (–1886).   An immigrant from Venezuela, he was the first Cuban planter to use electricity in his sugar mill outside of Cienfuegos in the mid to late 1800s. He amassed a fortune from sugar.

Father Felix Varela Morales (1788–1853).   He was a leading intellectual and nationalist. He supported self-rule and an end to slavery.

Diego Velázquez (–1524).   He was first Spanish governor of Cuba until his death in 1524.

Alfredo Zayas (1861–1934).   He was a member of the Liberal Party and president of the Republic of Cuba from 1921 to 1925.

Bibliographic Essay

The literature on the history of Cuba is unbelievably extensive and diverse. For scholars or those who want an overview of the past research on Cuba, I would initially suggest looking at Louis A. Pérez Jr.'s *Essays on Cuban History: Historiography and Research* (Gainesville: University Press of Florida, 1995) and Damain Fernandez's (ed.) *Cuban Studies since the Revolution* (Gainesville: University Press of Florida, 1992). For a general and scholarly historical overview, Hugh Thomas's *Cuba; the Pursuit of Freedom* (New York: Harper and Row, 1971) is meticulously researched, detailed and well written, although the general reader may find it rather lengthy at more than 1,500 pages. A more accessible history is Jaime Suchlicki's *Cuba: From Columbus to Castro*, 2nd ed. (Washington, D.C.: Pergamon-Brassey's, 1986). For a cultural history of Cuba focusing on its relationship with the United States, Louis A. Pérez Jr.'s *On Becoming Cuban* (Chapel Hill: University of North Carolina Press, 1999) is a masterful work that is already considered by many to be a classic.

For a study of the early history of Cuba, one should see Irene Wright's *The Early History of Cuba, 1492–1586* (New York: Macmillan, 1916). The edited book *Slaves, Sugar, and Colonial Society: Travel Accounts of Cuba, 1801–1899* (Wilmington, DE: Scholarly Resources, 1992) by Louis A. Pérez Jr. gives the reader insightful firsthand travel accounts of Cuban society in the 1800s. Another excellent scholarly study is Arthur Corwin's *Spain and the Abolition of Slavery in Cuba, 1817–1886* (Austin: University of Texas Press, 1967). For an overview that focuses on Cuba in the first part of the twentieth century, one should see Charles Chapman's *A History of the Cuban Republic* (New York: Macmillan, 1927) and Alan Dye's *Cuban Sugar in the Age of Mass Production: Technology and the Economy of the Sugar Central, 1899–1929* (Palo Alto, CA: Stanford University Press, 1998).

One should see Louis A. Pérez Jr.'s *Army Politics in Cuba, 1898–1958* (Pittsburgh: University of Pittsburgh Press, 1976) for the best scholarly study of the role of the military as it developed in twentieth-century Cuba and its role in the revolutionary upheavals of 1933 and 1959. For the best studies on the role of students in Cuba from the Generation of 1930 to the revolution, see Jaime Suchlicki's *University Students and Revolution in Cuba* (Coral Gables, FL: University of Miami Press, 1969) and Justo Carillo's *Cuba 1933: Students, Yankees and Soldiers* (Coral Gables, FL: University of Miami North-South Center, 1994). Another important book is Luis E. Aguilar's *Cuba 1933: Prologue to Revolution* (Ithaca, NY: Cornell University Press, 1972).

For books on the events that led to the fall of Fulgencio Batista, one of the most important books in recent years that draws on archival evidence previously unavailable is Julia Sweig's *Inside the Cuban Revolution* (Cambridge, MA: Harvard University Press, 2002). This book clearly supports the argument that the Cuban urban underground played just as much of a role in the revolution as Castro's guerrilla warfare in the countryside. In an earlier work that discusses the same theme, one should see Carlos Franqui's *Diary of the Cuban Revolution* (New York: Viking, 1980). Two other important books are Ernesto "Che" Guevara's *Episodes of the Cuban Revolutionary War, 1956–1958*, edited by Mary-Alice Waters (New York: Pathfinder, 1996) and *Revolutionary Struggle, 1947–1958*, vol. 1 of *The Selected Works of Fidel Castro*, edited by Rolando Bonachea and Nelson Valdes (Cambridge: MIT Press, 1972). Other books that discuss the historical events of the 1950s include Neil Mc-

Cauley's *A Rebel in Cuba: An American's Memoir* (Chicago: Quadrangle, 1970), Robert Tabor's *M-26: Biography of a Revolution* (New York: Lyle Stuart, 1961), Rufo Lopez-Fresquet's *My Fourteen Months with Castro* (New York: World Publishing, 1966) and Gladys Marel García-Pérez's *Insurrection and Revolution: Armed Struggle in Cuba, 1952–1959* (Boulder, CO: Rienner, 1998).

For studies that focus primarily on Cuba during the 1960s, one should see K. S. Karol's *Guerrillas in Power: The Course of the Cuban Revolution* (New York: Hill and Wang, 1970); Efran Cordova's *Castro and the Cuban Labor Movement: Statecraft and Strategy in a Revolutionary Period, 1959–1961* (Lanham, MD: University Press of America, 1987); Theodore Draper's *Castroism: Theory and Practice* (New York: Praeger, 1965) and *Castro's Revolution: Myths and Realities* (New York: Praeger, 1962); Andrés Suárez's *Cuba: Castroism and Communism* (Cambridge: MIT Press, 1967); Rene Dumont's *Socialism and Development* (New York: Grove, 1970); Richard Fagen's *The Transformation of Political Culture in Cuba* (Stanford, CA: Stanford University Press, 1969); Edward Gonzalez's *Cuba under Castro: The Limits of Charisma* (Boston: Houghton Mifflin, 1974); Carmelo Mesa-Lago's (ed.) *Revolutionary Change in Cuba* (Pittsburgh: University of Pittsburgh Press, 1971); Maurice Zeitlin's *Revolutionary Politics and the Cuban Working Class* (Princeton, NJ: Princeton University Press, 1967) and Mario Llerena's *The Unsuspected Revolution: The Birth and Rise of Castroism* (Ithaca, NY: Cornell University Press, 1978).

For other insightful overviews that emphasize the Castro years, one should see Juan M. Del Aguila's *Cuba: Dilemmas of a Revolution* (Boulder, CO: Westview, 1984) and Jorge I. Dominguez's *Cuba: Order and Revolution* (Cambridge, MA: Harvard University Press, 1978). For the two best scholarly analyses of the political economy of Cuba under Castro, one should see Susan Eva Eckstein's *Back from the Future* (Princeton, NJ: Princeton University Press, 1994) and Marifeli Pérez-Stable's *The Cuban Revolution: Origins, Course and Legacy* (New York: Oxford University Press, 1999). For a study in the relationship between the Catholic Church and the Cuban state, one should see John M. Kirk's *Between God and the Party* (Tampa: University of South Florida Press, 1989).

For an excellent study of the historical development of Havana, one should see Roberto Segre, Mario Coyula and Joseph Scarpaci's *Havana: Two Faces of the Antillean Metropolis* (New York: Wiley, 1997). James A. Michener and John King's *Six Days in Havana*

(Austin: University of Texas Press, 1989) is also recommended. One should also see M. Acosta and J. E. Hardoy's *Urban Reform in Revolutionary Cuba,* translated by M. Bochner (New Haven, CT: Yale University Press, 1973).

There are many biographies of Fidel Castro. Some tend to be overly sympathetic toward Castro and others highly antagonistic. Some of the better biographies include Robert Quirk's *Fidel Castro* (New York: Norton, 1993), Tad Szulc's *Fidel: A Critical Portrait* (New York: William Morrow, 1986), Lee Lockwood's *Castro's Cuba, Cuba's Fidel* (New York: Vintage, 1969), Enrique Meneses's *Fidel Castro* (New York: Taplinger, 1966) and Herbert Matthews's *Fidel Castro* (New York: Touchstone, 1969).

For a an excellent biography of Guevara, see Jorge Castaneda's *Companero: The Life and Death of Che Guevara* (New York: Knopf, 1997). Guevara wrote extensively and his most important readings include a compilation of his major writings on guerrilla warfare entitled *Guerrilla Warfare,* with an introduction by Marc Becker (Lincoln: University of Nebraska Press, 1998) and *Che Guevara on Revolution,* edited by Jay Mallin (Coral Gables, FL: University of Miami Press, 1969). *The Complete Bolivian Diaries of Che Guevara,* edited by Daniel James (New York: Cooper Square, 2000), is also recommended.

For a substantive and balanced study of the exile and immigrant Cuban community, one should see María Cristina García's *Havana USA* (Berkeley: University of California Press, 1996), and for a look at the Cuban American community and its relationship to the mass media, one should see Gonzalo R. Soruco's *Cubans and the Mass Media in South Florida* (Gainesville: University Press of Florida, 1996).

Cuba's relationship with the United States and the Soviet Union during the Cold War can be studied in many books, including James G. Blight, Bruce J. Allyn and David Welch's *Cuba on the Brink: Castro, the Missile Crisis and the Soviet Collapse* (New York: Pantheon, 1993); H. Michael Erisman's *Cuba's International Relations: The Anatomy of a Nationalistic Foreign Policy* (Boulder, CO: Westview, 1985); Laurence Chang and Peter Kornbluh's (eds.) *The Cuban Missile Crisis, 1962: A National Security Archive Documents Reader* (New York: New Press, 1992); Peter Wyden's *Bay of Pigs: The Untold Story* (New York: Simon and Schuster, 1979); Wayne Smith and Esteban Morales Dominguez's *Subject to Solution: Problems in Cuban-U.S. Relations* (Boulder, CO: Rienner, 1988); Donna

Rich Koplowitz's *Anatomy of a Failed Embargo: U.S. Sanctions against Cuba* (Boulder, CO: Rienner, 1998) and Sergio Díaz-Briquets's (ed.) *Cuban Internationalism in Sub-Saharan Africa* (Pittsburgh: Duquesne University Press, 1989).

There are a vast number of Web sites that deal with Cuba. I find that the most useful site is the Latin American Network Information Center at the University of Texas at http://lanic. utexas.edu/la/ca/cuba (accessed November 12, 2002). Another excellent and most informative site is the U.S.-Cuba Trade and Economic Council, which was established in 1994 and is perhaps the best website on how to do business in Cuba. It can be found at www.cubatrade.org (accessed November 12, 2002).

Index

About the Author

CLIFFORD L. STATEN is Associate Professor of Political Science and Dean of the School of Social Sciences at Indiana University Southeast.

Other Titles in the Greenwood Histories of the Modern Nations
Frank W. Thackeray and John E. Findling, Series Editors

The History of Argentina
Daniel K. Lewis

The History of Italy
Charles L. Killinger

The History of Australia
Frank G. Clarke

The History of Japan
Louis G. Perez

The History of Brazil
Robert M. Levine

The History of Mexico
Burton Kirkwood

The History of Canada
Scott W. See

The History of Nigeria
Toyin Falola

The History of China
David C. Wright

The History of Poland
M.B. Biskupski

The History of Congo
Didier Gondola

The History of Portugal
James M. Anderson

The History of France
W. Scott Haine

The History of Russia
Charles E. Ziegler

The History of Germany
Eleanor L. Turk

The History of Serbia
John K. Cox

The History of Holland
Mark T. Hooker

The History of South Africa
Roger B. Beck

The History of India
John McLeod

The History of Spain
Peter Pierson

The History of Iran
Elton L. Daniel

The History of Sweden
Byron J. Nordstrom

The History of Ireland
Daniel Webster Hollis III

The History of Turkey
Douglas A. Howard

The History of Israel
Arnold Blumberg